CW00822573

SONGS FOR SIVA

Vinaya Chaitanya was born in Muvattupuzha – the place of the three rivers – in the foothills of the Western Ghats, before the invasion of rubber plantations, in 1952. He met and was accepted as a disciple by Dr Nataraja Guru (1895–1973), disciple and successor of Narayana Guru, the philosopher-poet of Kerala.

He studied under Nataraja Guru in the gurukula, a worldwide contemplative community open to all. While serving his guru as head of the Narayana Gurukula Institute of Aesthetic Values in rural Bangalore for forty years, Vinaya was fortunate to learn Kannada from minstrels who introduced him to the vacana, kirtana and tatva forms of mystical poetry.

Vinaya has published books in Malayalam, Kannada and English. He now continues the wisdom-sharing tradition of the gurukula without institutional affiliation, treating the whole world as his gurukula (family of the guru).

SONGS FOR SIVA

Vacanas of Akka Mahadevi

Translated by

Vinaya Chaitanya

HARPER  PERENNIAL

NEW YORK · LONDON · TORONTO · SYDNEY · NEW DELHI

First published in India in 2017 by Harper Perennial
An imprint of HarperCollins *Publishers*

P-ISBN: 978-93-5264-410-0
E-ISBN: 978-93-5264-411-7

2 4 6 8 10 9 7 5 3 1

HarperCollins *Publishers*
A-75, Sector 57, Noida, Uttar Pradesh 201301, India
1 London Bridge Street, London, SE1 9GF, United Kingdom
Hazelton Lanes, 55 Avenue Road, Suite 2900, Toronto, Ontario M5R 3L2
and 1995 Markham Road, Scarborough, Ontario M1B 5M8, Canada
25 Ryde Road, Pymble, Sydney, NSW 2073, Australia
195 Broadway, New York, NY 10007, USA

Typeset in 10.5/13 Adobe Devanagari
by Jojy Philip, New Delhi

Printed and bound at
Thomson Press (India) Ltd

Foreword

H.S. Shivaprakash

Beautiful as jasmine but pointed like an arrow...

The vacanas of Akka Mahadevi – Karnataka's greatest treasure – were first made available throughout the English-speaking world thirty years ago, in the late A.K. Ramanujan's translations in *Speaking of Siva*. These were not the first translations, but the earlier ones were incapable of conveying Akka's tough lyricism to a non-Kannada readership. Ramanujan was able to capture successfully those aspects of his source texts that lent themselves to translation into the Anglo-American poetic language of the time. Despite the shortcomings of his translations, the unmistakable power of the original struck a chord in the hearts of the English-reading public both in India and in the West. Now, decades later, the time is ripe for a new translation of Akka's vacanas, for no single version can do justice to their many riches.

There are two major problems with the existing translations of these vacanas. The subject of Ramanujan's version is a spiritless body who resembles an accomplished athlete rather than Akka's hero, who can imbue the spirit with physical warmth. On the other hand, in their enthusiasm to communicate the spirit of the writings, translators before him impaired their corporeality; the protagonist who emerges from them is a disembodied god without face or flesh, devoid of all beauty and power. They interpreted Akka's vacanas as either scriptural or poetic texts. In fact they are neither. The twelfth-century saint poets of Karnataka held both scriptures and poetry in low esteem; indeed Adayya, a prolific poet of the period, considers both to be mere allegories. Those who believe in and live according to these allegories, says Adayya, are born of similes and die into similes. In short, vacana poets of Karnataka were aiming for something quite different from both the secular and the religious expression of their times. Because they believed deed (nade) to be embodiment of word (nudi), they mercilessly attacked all scripture and poetry that spoke of the imagined and idealized, and not of the experienced and lived truth. 'How can those who have known no suffering / feel the suffering of those in pain?' asks Akka in one of her vacanas.

I am indebted to Vinaya Chaitanya for asking me to write this foreword, a task made easier by his well-informed and lucid notes, which will give the intended (non-Kannadiga) reader a key to the mysteries of this treasure trove. Unlike his predecessors, Chaitanya is admirably receptive to the experiential dimensions of Akka's vacanas. Although he is alive to their socio-political nuances, his approach to them is above all a spiritual one. He has the open-minded humility of a genuine sadhak in the tradition of Narayana Guru of Kerala, who shared many of the socio-philosophical concerns of the twelfth-century saints of Karnataka, for instance, opposition to caste hierarchies and bigotry of all kinds. Chaitanya's non-Kannada background gives him the advantage of objectivity, while his engagement with and personal experience of sadhana enables him to appreciate the overpowering resonance of Akka's words. He shows, moreover, an acute awareness of textual issues that never bothered earlier translators.

Most important of all, he has understood the multifacetedness of the original texts, for Akka's compositions are poetic without being poetry, spiritual without being religious or scriptural. This crucial awareness informs his work even when the nuances of the words cannot be conveyed in translation. Whenever the word 'Channamallikarjuna' appears here, for example, it bears the suffix 'jasmine-tender'. But this tenderness is only one attribute of Akka's hero: he also has the brute strength of Arjuna, indefatigable archer. Akka describes herself as 'a woman only in name'. In her longing for and union with her Cosmic Hero, Channamallikarjuna – beautiful as jasmine but hard and pointed like an arrow – she has lost her sexual identity, the basis of all dualisms. Though Chaitanya does not bring this out in his translation, the overall perception and selection of vacanas is informed by deep understanding of this essential point.

Let me conclude by sharing what I consider to be the essence of Akka's unique vacanas. 'One has the here, another the hereafter, / One has no here, another no hereafter. / Another has neither here nor hereafter. / Those who have taken refuge in Channamallikarjuna, jasmine-tender, have both the here and the hereafter.' With these words, she offers the world what it has found and lost over and over again: the awesome courage of lifelong surrender, something that has eluded materialists and spiritualists, theists, atheists and agnostics alike. Akka's words embody and act out an inextinguishable love that is found only through self-effacement. It is precise and to the point, unlike that vague, universal love which seeks to love all despite being unable to love any one being. Neither is it limited, like the various forms of individual and collective selfish love that prevail in the world today. It is an intense vision and experience of the source of all love and all longing that alone can quench the thirst for all forms of thirst. It is entirely unlike the dukkha of Buddhism, the maya of Vedanta or the sin of Christianity. It is that naked primeval desire which is the mother of all desire. It burns and pines with love and throbs with irrepressible expectation. It is Channamallikarjuna, the name Akka gave to her path of Siva, where heaven and hell become one in the clear understanding of continuous awareness, turning nectar and poison into each other. For, in the true path of Siva, as Acharya Utpaladeva said, even poison turns into nectar and misery to joy.

The image of Akka that emerged in earlier translations is of a radical woman poet prefiguring many of the concerns of present-day feminism. The image of our own age as reflected in Akka's vacanas is accurate as far as it goes, but there are important differences. The experience of the sacred – precisely what our age has lost sight of – is the very breath of Akka's vacanas, and Vinaya Chaitanya is to be commended for bringing this aspect of the author to the fore. There is little doubt that his labour of love will appeal to a wide readership, for in Akka's vacanas is Siva's plenty. Students and practitioners of literature, history, sociology, women's studies, philosophy and religion are sure to find Akka's vacanas fascinating in many different ways, while these vacanas are of great significance also to true spiritual seekers everywhere. In an age teeming with half-baked and imperfect gurus, the authentic and enduring voice of Akka the great Sivaguru can bring greater light and shaktipat, transmission of energy, to a world in which both are in short supply.

H.S. Shivaprakash.
Chaitra Pournima, Vasanta Masa, Svabhanu Samvatsara

Translator's Introduction

VINAYA CHAITANYA

*United like word and meaning are Parvati and
    Paramesvara,
The twin parents of the universe; them I adore*

With these opening lines from Kalidasa's *Raghuvamsa*,
let us invoke the blessings of our prime parents in order
to find meaning not only of words, but also of life itself –
the meaning of all meanings.

Background

Siva – sometimes seen sitting alone in silent
contemplation on snowy peaks, sometimes less austerely
under a spreading banyan tree surrounded by disciples
both human and animal – is always portrayed facing
south; hence he is sometimes called Dakshinamurti,
the South-facing Lord. In the south, at the extreme
tip of peninsular India where oceans meet, stands
Kanyakumari, the Virgin Goddess, meditating on her
lover-lord, the crescent-wearing madman of the north.

It is between these extremities – the snowy peaks
of Kailas and the watery depths of the southern
oceans – that the poetry of Indian spirituality has its
being. The extremes can also be seen as representing
the ambivalence present in human knowledge itself:

between concepts and percepts, names and forms, mind and matter, male and female and all such antinomies. These poles cancel each other out in a poetic upsurge that fills consciousness completely, eliminating the duality of the knowing subject and the known object.

It is the dialectics between male and female that makes for the creative evolution of the world. When these opposites are united in harmony, there is peace and contentment; when the balance between them is lost, there is suffering. Different degrees of participation could produce various degrees of union or separation. The concept of ardhanarisvara, the half-man, half-woman deity, describes the most unitive state, in which female and male are the inseparable left and right halves of the same body. (The yin–yang of the Chinese too stands for this intimate indivisibility of the negative and positive principles of nature.)

One could also think of one's own consciousness as alternating between an instinctual point of departure and an aspirational or ideal end point; between this alpha and omega a circulation of values takes place. The closer the actual and the ideal are, the happier one is. Resolution of the basic conflict between the two, which makes life problematic to most of us, has been the aim of the numerous philosophical and mystical traditions of the world. How far each has succeeded can be judged only from within, by the system's own unique yet universal norms. We must also remember that each system was a product of a particular time and its needs.

Varied as these traditions may be, all have produced

poetry of the highest quality – a natural result of the search for verbal expression of states of being from which 'words recoil, together with the mind, not able to reach it', as the Upanishads put it. Poetry infuses words with spirit, trying to embody the ultimate silence where word and meaning cancel each other out in the transcendent experience, within contemplative consciousness, of poetic meaning or value.

In the Upanishads, the poet-seer is identified with the Absolute Godhead. Christian theology allows man to say that he is created in the image of God: 'the Kingdom of God is within you', that 'you can be perfect even as your Father in Heaven is perfect' or that 'the Word was with God and the Word was God'. Indian traditions assert with equal boldness that 'You are That; I myself am He', and that 'the knower of the Absolute becomes the Absolute'. The equality in these existential statements endeavours to give tangible meaning to the notion of the Absolute, more popularly known as God. Such meaning must be a universal value, otherwise it will have no significance for purposeful human living. It can only be in this sense that 'a thing of beauty is a joy forever'. A thing must exist, must be known and must have intrinsic value. Existence, consciousness and value are three categories or perspectives from which the real is apprehended in the Upanishads. In Sanskrit, they are called satcidananda. Satyam, sivam, sundaram (the true, the good, the beautiful) are used in Saivite traditions. We find the same categories in Plato.

From the Tirukkural of Thiruvalluvar in Tamil; the

works of Kalidasa; the hymns of Sankara; the poems of Kabir; Tukaram, Jnaneswar and other great devotees of the Marathas; the poetic genius of Allama Prabhu and Akka Mahadevi; right down to the most recent utterances of Sri Ramakrishna, Vivekananda, Tagore and Narayana Guru, the golden thread continues, always trying to give meaning to the notion of the ultimate. This ultimate can be thought of theologically as a god or goddess, psychologically as the self, or cosmologically as the universe or the All. The urge towards union itself must be understood as a dynamism, alternately touching the loftiest heights or the most earthy depths of value worlds or visions.

Envisioning beauty necessarily brings up the 'form' of beauty, the beautiful. To the man, the form of absolute beauty is that of woman, and vice versa. This is where the erotic-mystical enters poetry. The poems of St John of the Cross, Rumi and Attar, the Song of Songs, may all be profitably studied in this context. The *Saundarya Lahari* and *Sivananda Lahari* of Sankara, the *Gita Govinda* of Jayadeva, 'Kali Natakam' and other poems on the eternal feminine by Narayana Guru, the *Syamala-dandakam* and *Kumarasambhava* of Kalidasa, all belong in the same highly charged category. Study of these will help us to understand the eternal and universal significance of the life and teachings of Akka Mahadevi and to place her in context. It is regrettable indeed that we have lost the names of most of the women gurus through the vicissitudes of history, but fortunate that some of their poetic genius has been preserved.

The proper theme of all poetry, or even art, could be said to be love. Poetry must be pleasing or beautiful. In Indian poetic traditions, mysticism and the wisdom that goes with it have never been separated from the beauty of poetry. Aesthetics, ethics, economics and all other disciplines that involve human well-being can be blended into a symphonic whole that consoles or elevates the spirit. Thus, poetry in India has always had the serious purpose of revealing the ultimate. It is wisdom – the finalized knowledge or certitude that we can have about our own feelings and thoughts – that is the subject matter as well as the object of poetry. It is in this context of perpetual wisdom that we must place Akka Mahadevi as a poet of the universal aspiration for union with the All, whom she visualized as Channamallikarjuna, the Jasmine-tender Lord.

To those who may find all this detour from the pure or devotional poems of Akka unnecessary, I can do no better than point to the very first of the poems, in which she refers to her Lord who 'hides as the being behind becoming'. Bomma (from Brahman) and bhava are the words that she uses; and they must be recognized as belonging to the idiom of a perennial philosophy, which she would not have used unconsciously.

Introduction

Akka Mahadevi is one of the brightest luminaries of the Virasaiva movement, which flourished in Karnataka in the twelfth century under the high-minded inspiration of devotees like Basavanna and poet-seers like Allama

Prabhu who were moved by great compassion towards fellow beings oppressed by ignorance and misery. Such seers evoked the archetypal Siva-father image, ever vibrant in the recesses of primal memory, to speak out against those perverted customs that, in the name of piety and holiness, polluted the pure springs of wisdom. Vehemently opposed to everything that divided the family of humankind – be it caste, sex, language or dress – they established model communities which transcended the social barriers foisted on the common people by decadent theocracies and corrupt monarchies. There were many women seers, too, at the forefront of the movement.

Ironically, like a physician who contracts some dreaded disease in his efforts to cure the sick, this magnificent effort against the divisive walls of caste, gender and language has itself succumbed to the very ills that it set out to cure, and has been co-opted by vested interests. It would be outside the scope of this introduction to go into the question of caste, which continues to gnaw at Indian society from within. The caste system was a bold theoretical attempt to classify psychological types that failed miserably, at tremendous cost to culture, and we must decry its perversions as wholly inhuman and without any social or spiritual basis. A parallel in the West is the horror of the Inquisition. The point made here is that unilateral theories which exclude large sections of humankind cannot claim universal relevance. Spiritual aspiration must always be committed and inclusive, not limited by selfish preferences. The closed and static loyalties of clan, caste, tribe, sect and nation all have to be transcended before one can embark on open and dynamic ways of life. As a flood could contain within itself wells and ponds from the affected area, this transcendence is not a violent phenomenon. Not destroying, but fulfilling, as Jesus said.

As human beings, we each find ourselves in a defined value system. We are exhorted to love the Lord God by loving our neighbour as our self. Seen in this way, spirituality seeks to clarify the relation between the individual (who inhabits a world of plurality and relativity) and the totality of the universal situation around him or her. As 'happiness' underlies all spiritual striving, it is in the context of what benefits all humankind that the high value of God must be understood. Atheists too are bound by the need to establish and affirm the day-to-day transactions that bind people to their fellow beings. Akka's poetry consistently maintains the strict bipolarity of self and God through such human qualities as generosity, open-mindedness and adoration.

'That in lightning which makes a person gasp and says "Ah!", that is the Absolute,' says the *Kena* Upanishad. The same Upanishad describes an event of special significance at this stage of our discussion. The Vedic gods of Fire and Wind, Agni and Vayu, along with their chief Indra, come face to face with the Absolute, which appears to them in the form of a mysterious being that they cannot comprehend. Eventually, 'in that very space' appears an 'exceedingly beautiful woman, Uma, daughter of the Snowy Mountains', who explains the being to them. We are reminded that Dante needed a Beatrice to lead him to the higher worlds. The role of the feminine in revealing the nature of the Absolute is thus clear to us from both Eastern and Western traditions.

In Akka's vacanas there is no attempt to explain away any normal human concern. In fact, Akka and her jasmine-tender lover together comprise all the attitudes that go to make up human nature generally. All psychic states, both positive and negative, are in force and only enhance the totality of the value dynamics between them. It is by transcending good and bad, not by denying them, or by just trying to be good in a one-sided sense, that perfection is to be sought: in the search itself, by itself, through itself. Jealousy in love is said to be incompatible with pure love. At the same time, one is asked to love one's God with all one's heart in all the world's spiritual traditions. This necessarily implies exclusion of all that is extraneous to the dialectics of the affiliation. An example may serve to make this clearer: imagine a pond with hundreds of lotus flowers in it. The lotus is known for its love of the sun; its flowers open only when touched by the rays of the rising sun and close at sunset. Although there are many lotuses in the pond, each has a unique personal relationship with the sun, the source of light. The traditions also speak of the lotus of the heart, which is similarly placed in relation to a supreme sun risen in the firmament of consciousness. The lotuses are also related organically to each other at their roots.

The life of Akka Mahadevi

Little is known about Akka's life. Ever engaged in seeking the eternal as distinct from the transient, Indians have never cared much for history, finding their needs met by mythology. If you believe Akka Mahadevi to be an incarnation of the Goddess, what need is there for a birth certificate? This much can be gathered from legends: Mahadevi was born in Udutadi, in the Shivamoga district of Karnataka, in the twelfth century. Her parents were devout adherents of the Virasaiva movement, and she naturally followed. Initiated into Siva worship at the age of twelve, she would spend all her time in playful veneration of the village temple deity, Channamallikarjuna, a form of Siva. Channa means 'beautiful'; mallika is jasmine; arjuna, meaning 'bright' or 'white', was also the name of the great warrior disciple of the *Bhagavadgita*. According to legend, Arjuna fought Siva on order to obtain a potent weapon from him. The Goddess turned all the arrows that Arjuna shot into jasmine flowers, so that Siva was covered in jasmines; thus he acquired the name Mallikarjuna. The intervention of the Goddess as a neutralizing influence in a war between man and god is to be noted. Equally important is the conjoining of the delicate and fragrant jasmine with the image of Arjuna, the greatest warrior in Indian mythology. As stressed throughout this introduction, the merging of polar opposites in the neutrality of an absolute, constant value which can be verified only by personal experience is the key to contemplation. The image of God needs salvaging from the thunderbolt-wielding, punishing presences found at various Olympian heights. 'God Is Love', hence the translation here of Channamallikarjuna as 'jasmine-tender'.

Mahadevi considered herself wedded to Siva and grew up into a very beautiful woman. The local king Kaushika saw her and fell in love with her, and sent emissaries to her parents to seek her hand in marriage. But Kaushika was a Jain and the parents were reluctant. When the king threatened to kill them, Mahadevi grudgingly agreed to the marriage, albeit on three conditions:

I will spend time meditating on the Lord as I please.
I will spend time in the company of other devotees
    as I please.
I will spend time attending to the service of the
    guru as I please.

If the king went against these three conditions, she would leave him.

Once, when Mahadevi was asleep, a sage from afar arrived at the palace. When attendants came to inform the queen, the king sent them away without waking Mahadevi; but she awoke and, telling the king that two more promises remained, went to receive the sage. On another occasion, Kaushika, seeing Mahadevi seated in meditation, was sexually aroused and went to embrace her. Rising, disturbed, she reminded the king that he had just one more promise to break before she could be free.

One night, Mahadevi's guru came to the palace. In her eagerness to greet him she jumped out of bed and ran to the guru, who said, 'Go and get dressed and come, my dear.' She returned to the bedroom but the king, angrily abusing her, refused to let her have her clothes, saying, 'Why do you need clothes, great devotee that you are?' Mahadevi, telling the king that he had violated all three conditions of their agreement, left the palace with only her tresses to cover her.

It is worth remembering that in some Jain traditions the contemplatives or ascetics are naked digambaras (sky-clad). Siva devotees too, quite indifferent to social norms of respectability, let their hair become matted in imitation of their wild God (evoking images of Dionysus, Robert Bly's Iron John and even hippies). Long hair also hides the 'person' behind the appearance, as Dasimayya poignantly says in a famous vacana:

If long hair and breasts come, they say 'woman',
If moustache and beard come, they say 'man',
The Self within, is it woman or man, O Ramanatha?

There are as many scholars, both ancient and modern, who refute that Akka was ever married as those who believe she was, but all agree on her having had to deal with Kaushika, a Jaina chieftain. The Virasaiva movement had to face a theocratic orthodoxy on the one hand, and Jain heterodoxy on the other. The fact that Akka walked around as a digambari may denote that she was able to achieve in her own person some sort of synthesis of these rival traditions. Anyway, she makes use of the highest model of Jain spirituality.

Akka means 'older sister'. Mahadevi was addressed as such by Allama himself, after he had been convinced of the genuineness of her experiences. Basavanna calls her 'the mother who gave me birth', thus according her the highest honour. Reverential references to her are found in much of the vacana literature. Whole works, medieval as well as modern, deal with her life and teachings. Interestingly, no mention is made of her by any of the other women writers of her time.

Having lived for a time in the company of all the great devotees of the Lord, Akka sought, and obtained, their permission to retire to Srisaila, a holy mountain where the Jasmine-tender One awaited her. She walked into the banana grove there, never to be seen again. Her path, from the 'alone to the Alone' leading from her parental home to her Mount Carmel in Srisaila – via the palace of the husband-king, and the illustrious assembly of those who have found refuge in the Lord – reverberates all the way with her songs. Different stages and encounters can be recognized in them; some feel familiar, some strange.

The Vacanas

The vacana literary form arose as a part of the people's movement against the oppression in the name of Sanskrit as the 'divine' language. The Virasaiva poets wrote in Kannada, refuting the millennia-old belief that 'native' languages were incapable of dealing with universal verities. The word vacana does not mean 'poem' at all. Literally it means 'to give one's word', 'to make a promise or a commitment'. Most vacana poets were no respecters of the poetic rules of scale and metre. The first known vacana poet is the tenth-century weaver Dasimayya. The beginnings of such indigenous literary effort must also be traced to Jain poets who used a mixture of Sanskrit and Kannada, a tradition known as campu.

It is usual to see the vacana movement as part of the bhakti cults that began to spring up in India during the eighth century AD. This is only partly true. India at that time was a melting pot of different cultural and religious traditions. Islam had arrived. Casteist theocracies had made use of the intellectual brilliance of Sankara to defeat the noble challenge of Buddhism. There were numerous popular movements, some having their roots in the genuine aspirations of the people, others manipulated to stop the downtrodden from flocking to take advantage of the equality promised by the new religions. Virasaivism was not just a reactionary impulse; rather it was an appeal to an earlier stratum of spirituality. Thus it was a continuation of similar efforts made time and again since the Vedic subjugation of an older, more contemplative tradition associated with Siva, himself known as akula, 'belonging to no family'. The reference to the pre-Aryan and Aryan must be seen only in the context of understanding the 'challenge and response' in spiritual traditions, and not in any narrow racial sense. To avoid any such confusion, let us also add here that there are no pure Aryans or Dravidians in present-day India.

Virasaivism was unique in the equal status it accorded to the sexes. This, it must be remembered, is what made a Mahadevi Akka possible – not just her, but many others like her: there are thirty-three vacanakartis (women writers of vacanas) whose poems are available. Such equality applied not only in the matter of literary creation, which is a speciality, but in all aspects of daily life. Menstruating women, for instance, were not considered 'unclean' and could attend worship like all the others. How revolutionary that was becomes clear when we realize that in most Indian villages even today the 'unclean' woman must sleep outdoors. (Of course, they generally work so hard that the week's banishment must be a respite.)

A fine and scholarly introduction to the vacanas and to Virasaivism in general can be found in A.K. Ramanujan's *Speaking of Siva* (Harmondsworth: Penguin, 1973), which also contains selections from the works of Dasimayya, Basavanna, Akka and Allama, four stalwarts of the movement.

To return to her story, the sky-clad Akka came before the 'auspicious' assembly of devotees at Kalyana, presided over by Allama Prabhu and Basavanna. Searching questions were put to her by the master poet – seer Allama – all of which she answered with the conviction arising from her own deep experience of the numinous within. For example, Allama asked her why, if she had outgrown the need for clothes, she had covered herself with her hair. She answered, 'Unless the fruit is ripe the peel won't come off; seeing the insignia of the god of love on my body might trouble you, I thought, so I covered myself.' Both the question and the answer are well-known vacanas. They are exemplary in their terse suggestiveness and their layers of meaning that conceal still deeper meanings.

Most of the vacanas are responses to questions or situations and, as such, are best read in their complete context (as found in the *Sunyasampadane* texts); even in Kannada, let alone in translations, their full meaning can be hard to discern. That something comes through in at least some of the poems, despite the many difficulties in the translator's way, vouches for their eternal place in the discourse of wisdom. My work on the vacanas has been laborious indeed, and but for the joy of finding such rare jewels, I would have given up long ago.

I cannot claim to have done Akka full justice, but I can say with all humility that I have tried my best to bring out the feeling of the original, often sacrificing readability in the interests of loyalty to the poet's choice of images and phrases. The textual variants in different sources have sometimes been an obstacle: on occasion the same vacana can be given two exactly opposite meanings just by the adding or taking away of a single word. Vacana 41 contains a typical example. Beginning:

Once you have eaten the fruit,
Does it matter who prunes the tree?

Akka goes on to ask, after some vivid analogies,

> Once Channamallikarjuna, jasmine-tender,
> Is known, does it matter whether
> The body is eaten by dogs or rots in water?

Now, it is possible to read the same passage as:

> Once Channamallikarjuna, jasmine-tender,
> Is not known, does it matter whether
> The body is eaten by dogs or rots in water?

Both are correct and plausible, and both are found in different editions of the Kannada texts; the two versions exist in the oral tradition as well. But not all texts give the alternative reading. While in the original just the addition or omission of the syllable *ya* in the verb meaning 'to know' – arida and ari-ya-da – makes all the difference, I have thought it best not to deprive the reader of both possibilities, and have rendered it as 'Is (not) known'. Admittedly it looks awkward, but giving the alternative in a footnote could affect one's initial understanding of the meaning. Such considerations have been always in my mind, and you will find other examples.

I have sometimes found it impossible to render the whole dialectics – of words and sense – in the translation and have had to make do with second best. Vacana 28 may be cited here:

> I begged of every plant to sustain the body,
> They gave from the bounty of their being.
> Begging, I was caught in becoming;
> Giving, they became devotees

In the original, the sustenance craved is for the body, anga, and the plants give forth from their linga. Not only do the two words sound alike, they are dialectical pairs: anga is the gross body while linga is the causal body. Savouring the homogenous essence of both together, linga–anga sama rasa, is the goal of spiritual effort in the tradition. In the last two lines, getting caught in becoming, bhavi, has its dialectical counterpart in bhakta, the devotee. The original words convey all this in themselves, and are fully understood by the reader or listener, while the hapless translator is left to do the best he can. But despite the difficulties involved, I have enjoyed my ten years' work on these vacanas and hope to have passed on some of the great inspiration that they have been to me.

Terminology and usage

A brief explanation of the concepts guru, linga and jangama is in order, as they recur often in the text and are fundamental to the Virasaiva philosophy. Guru embodies a double negative in that it means literally 'that which dispels darkness'. We know that light alone can dispel darkness. Why then is it not stated directly? This question brings us up against a characteristic feature of the language of mysticism: the negative way or nivritti marga. It is through a process of reducing external phenomena that we come to the numinous core within, from where we can build outwards. More particularly, the guru principle stands for the ultimate vision achieved in the context of wisdom communication, while the disciple's earnestness in searching is the starting point. The affiliation to the guru saves the seeker from being a victim of the delusions and hallucinations of his own mind. That the guru is a relinquisher ensures that he has no selfish motives, and is thus interested solely in guiding the disciples to their own inner sanctum. Sharing wisdom 'blesseth him that gives and him that takes', as Shakespeare so tellingly said of the quality of mercy.

The guru initiates the disciple into the 'secrets' of wisdom (secrets only in that they are not seen or recognized by all). In the Virasaiva tradition, the guru initiating the disciple gives him a linga, literally a symbol. The Sivalinga, the phallic stone image, is a much misunderstood item of Indian iconography. A vertical scale of values is what is implied, sometimes represented by a pillar of light, a jyotir-linga.

There is also the story of how Brahma and Visnu, taking the form of a swan and a boar respectively, fly up and dive down to find the ends of a column of light, a manifestation of Siva. For all we know they are still at it, as the vertical series of values represented by the pillar of light, is endless. Thus the miniature linga that the guru gives to the initiate stands for all life values in the context of self-realization. It can also be seen as a symbol of the self or soul of the aspirant. It is important to note that one is not born a Virasaivite but becomes one only after initiation by a guru.

Jangama (literally 'one who comes and goes') is the mendicant devotee. Philosophically, it is the opposite of sthavara, the static or fixed. Whereas the stone linga is firmly fixed, the aspirant who has been duly instructed in the teachings moves about freely, and is worthy of worship as one in whom the word has met its own meaning. Jesus also tells us to 'become a passer-by'.

Akka and I

I first came across the vacanas in the oral tradition to which they really belong. There are still a number of 'minstrels' in our villages who sing the vacanas. Many of them are unlettered but can sing hundreds of songs literally 'by heart'. Listening to some of these songs, I could discern the vague outline of that very path on which these poems reverberate. They echo in the caverns of my own heart as I stumble upon the tail end of it, and I cannot help gasping 'Ah!' Hence these translations, and the more personal nature of what follows.

It may not be out of place here to go a little into the Narayana Gurukula tradition to which I belong. Founded in 1923 by Nataraja Guru (1895–1973), disciple and successor of Narayana Guru (1854–1928), the Gurukula is a worldwide contemplative community dedicated to self-realization and world citizenship. Its motto is the maxim voiced by Narayana Guru: 'Humanity is of one caste, of one religion and of one God.' (The words 'race', 'faith' and 'goal' could be used instead of 'caste', 'religion' and 'God' to convey the meaning more broadly.) The Gurukula is open to all regardless of class, religion, sex, language, nationality or other divisions.

That *Homo sapiens* is one species needs no argument

to establish. That religion is also one may require some explanation. We can do no better than to quote Narayana Guru: 'Every person at all times makes effort in every way, aiming at self-happiness; understand this to be the one religion of the world.' This self must be understood as a universal concrete, abstracted and generalized so as to be free from all limitations of name and form. Just as all shades of the colour green can be seen in different leaves, it is also possible to understand the colour in the abstract, free of any leaf. To quote Narayana Guru again, 'What we know here as this man or that, reflection reveals to be the Self's prime form; conduct aimed at securing one's own happiness must at the same time result in the happiness of the other.' Thus it is that the seer is moved to act always with the general good in view. No one would dispute that, of all that is dear to a person, nothing is dearer than his or her own self, since it is only with reference to oneself that anything can be of value. One's own well-being is inextricably linked with the well-being of all, and this realization brings about a giving up of all that is detrimental to the general good. It is in this sense that sannyasa, renunciation, must be understood. It is not in any way to be confused with notions of holiness or institutional pomp.

The *Isa* Upanishad unequivocally connects God and the world when it says, 'The Lord (Isa) abides in all this, whatever there is in this moving world.' One could also place universal personal happiness as the common goal of all, abolishing all duality of ends and means. Such a goal as a high value could replace the word 'God' for those who have trouble with it, making it possible to remain in a neutral state between belief and scepticism, and doing away with the need to divide the human family into believers and infidels. No one, even an atheist, could claim total indifference to values.

This explanation should make it easier to understand the Gurukula as an educational rather than a religious institution. Its founder Nataraja Guru, while being a disciple of a Guru in the context of perennial wisdom-transmission, was also a trained scientist. Sent by Narayana Guru to Europe to familiarize himself with the best that Western traditions could offer, Nataraja Guru was awarded the D.Litt. with triple honours by the Sorbonne University in 1933 for his thesis 'The Personal Factor in the Educative Process'. He travelled extensively, founding gurukulas in different parts of the world.

We have already seen that the gurus of humanity are moved by their great compassion to re-evaluate and restate the enduring and fundamental verities in terms of their own times. Most of their fellow beings are far too involved in the need of the hour to be able to gain a glimpse of the eternal. It thus becomes imperative for the benevolent seer to interpret his or her grand vision so that the moment may be correctly understood as the meeting point of past aspirations and future possibilities. Otherwise, life loses its dignity of purpose and degenerates (as it usually does) into 'ignoble strife'. The most familiar example of re-evaluation is Jesus's oft repeated, 'You have heard it said … but, verily, verily, I say unto you'. We find Akka on many occasions saying, 'O brothers who argue about ... listen.'

Narayana Guru, in his *Scriptures of Mercy*, equates grace, love and mercy with the unitive value of compassion or kindliness that underlies all the world's religions and philosophies, citing all the known teachers and prophets as exemplars of this one single value. In the India of Narayana Guru's time, caste and religious rivalry was the most damaging problem that needed attention. He exposed it theoretically through his writings, showing how such inhuman practices were not sanctioned in the scriptures or according to common sense, and he founded model communities transcending all barriers.

Following the same lines, Nataraja Guru recognized the need to bring science and philosophy together – a need he felt all the more keenly as a result of his extensive sojourns in Europe between and after the two world wars. The one-sided growth of the physical sciences, which gradually appropriated the very word *science*, was a reaction to the earlier one-sidedness of the church. Both needed correction 'to normalize and re-normalize' themselves in terms of each other, as Nataraja Guru would say.

Nataraja Guru developed and used a proto-linguistic structuralism based on the Cartesian coordinates that underlie wisdom literature the world over. The *Mandukya* Upanishad even says, 'this self is four-limbed', meaning that the structure of consciousness consists of the four states of waking, dreaming, deep sleep and the transcendent (the last called simply 'the fourth' because it is beyond thought or word). The four states are also referred to as the actual, virtual, causal and ultimate. The first two make up a horizontal world of paradox and multiplicity, while the last two make up a vertical scale of unitive values. In fact this is merely a two-dimensional description of a dynamism which must be understood from within, intuitively, as consciousness or awareness itself must be. This structure, then, becomes capable of containing all possible value-visions and apparently irreconcilable systems by assigning each its proper place. Nataraja Guru developed from it an 'integrated science of the absolute' in which physics and metaphysics or science and poetry lend support to and verify each other.

Elaborating on particular applications of this science of unitive values, Guru wrote manifestos on 'One-world Education', 'One-world Economics', 'Ethics', 'Aesthetics', 'Unified Science', etc. He also translated and commented on the major works of Narayana Guru and on the *Saundarya Lahari* of Sankara, a masterpiece of structuralism on erotic mystisicm, the subject matter of all genuine poetry. It was while he was teaching, translating and commenting on this last text, which he translates as 'Upsurging Billow of Beauty', that chance brought me to him, or, less egoistically speaking, the grace of the Goddess brought us together. (Guru would say, 'Bring in the God too, so that the god and the goddess may cancel each other out. Don't be one-sided. By cancelling them out, you get a neutral unitive value.')

You could call it whatever you liked – truth, goodness, beauty. What mattered was that the wonder intoxicated you, freed you, giving you the peace that 'passeth understanding'.

I have gone into all this at some length so that the reader may share something of my own interest and background in contemplating the vacana literature. As stated earlier, vacana means 'commitment', 'a word given'. According to Nataraja Guru, the Gurukula is based on 'unlimited liability'. Kula, as in Gurukula, means 'family'. 'From each according to his ability, to each according to his need', 'All for one and one for all' were among the guidelines he cited for students.

Even though I had no more than a smattering of Kannada when I first encountered the vacanas, the content of at least some of them was not unfamiliar. This brings us back once more to the universal poet-singer tradition of the seers and their wisdom. Thus, it is not as a stranger that I have approached the vacanas but as a humble disciple of the perennial lineage of the guru tradition, understood independently of its historic and geographic peculiarities which are incidental and only secondary to the pure wisdom content. Even the names of the gurus are relevant only in so far as they exemplify, in their own persons, this wisdom of the universal self – and are of supreme value to the seeker. Even now there are many gurus, simple women and men who represent this wisdom in and through their own lives. That most of them remain unrecognized by the world does not detract from their personal importance. They contribute more to world peace than the armies of all nations put together. Rural Karnataka still fosters this priceless tradition.

The vacanas have been very helpful to me in connection with caste as it exists in the villages around us. Untouchability, though illegal, is still observed. In my encounters with caste I have found a tremendous source of support in the openness of the vacanas, which give my words validity when I quote Narayana Guru on the absurdity of the caste system. All these factors have shaped my understanding of the vacanas.

My work on the vacanas began when Nitya (Guru Nitya Chaitanya Yati), who succeeded Nataraja Guru, found a number of them in an English translation and asked me to translate some from Kannada into Malayalam. As these Dravidian languages are first cousins, I was able to make a much closer rendering than was available in English. Nitya liked the translations and asked me to continue, in both Malayalam and English. He was very happy to hear that the translations were arousing interest and, but for his failing health, would have introduced them himself. He was looking forward to seeing them published when, in May 1999, he merged back into the Unmanifest. However, on our last day together, in response to a three-line verse of my own, he wrote the vacana

May the tender dew-drop
In the jasmine bud
Protect us.

Bowing in profound adoration before the wisdom and love of the Absolute, which is the sum total of us all, this book is dedicated to you, beloved reader.

1

Like treasure hidden by the earth,
Like taste hidden by the fruit,
Like gold hidden by the stone,
Like oil hidden by the sesame seed,
Like fire hidden by the wood,
Channamallikarjuna, jasmine-tender,
Hides as the being behind becoming;
No one knows him.

Channamallikarjuna: one of the names of Siva; see Introduction.
being: the Absolute, bomma (from Brahman).
becoming: bhava, the phenomenal cycle of birth and death.

2

When I did not know myself
Where were you, tell me?
Like the colour in gold,
You were in me.
Though you were in me,
I saw you as different,
O Channamallikarjuna, Jasmine-tender!

🌿

Colour in gold: totally inseparable.

3

Maya has troubled the body as shadow,
Troubled breath as the mind,
Troubled mind as memory,
Troubled memory as awareness,
Troubled awareness as forgetfulness,
With a firm sceptre,
Maya rules the many worlds.
O Channamallikarjuna, jasmine-tender,
Who will overcome the maya
You have spread?

4

If I say I have left maya
Maya won't leave;
If I don't leave maya
It will ride on my back.
To the yogi maya became a yogini,
To the ascetic maya became
A female ascetic,
To the one with self-control
Maya become a flatterer.
I won't be scared of your maya,
Channamallikarjuna, jasmine-tender,
I swear by you.

One with self-control: yati, a renunciant, sannyasi, from yama, 'restraint'.

5

Please cut away the delusion of my maya,
Take away the darkness of my body,
Please remove the restlessness of my spirit;
Channamallikarjuna, jasmine-tender,
May your grace loosen
The bonds of the world
That bind me.

6

When I say I have seen,
Seeing becomes a veil,
If I say I am united,
The mood becomes veil,
What shall I say and how?
If I say I know
Forgetfulness becomes a veil.
How can I overcome your maya?
Save me!
Channamallikarjuna, jasmine-tender.

The state of union is beyond all description, beyond all subject–object duality.

7

Stream behind, river ahead,
Which is the way?
Lake behind, trap ahead,
Which is easy? Please tell.
The maya you have spread
Is killing.
Save me! Save me, do!
Channamallikarjuna, jasmine-tender.

8

The buffalo has one worry,
The cobbler has another;
The righteous one has one worry,
The evil-doer has another;
I have my own worry,
You have the worry of your desires!
No, go, let go my clothes, you fool!
I am worried that
Channamallikarjuna, jasmine-tender,
Won't be pleased with me!

A vacana addressed to Akka's husband Kaushika.
The righteous one ... the evil-doer: dharmi and karmi (doer).

9

If you jump into the sea
Carrying a stone
Will your troubles be over, O mother?
If, even after eating, you say you are hungry,
I'll say 'Too bad'.
If the mind burns at every place seen
How will the husband, Channamallikarjuna,
    jasmine-tender,
Be pleased, O mother?

10

Lord, see, my mind touches you
Yet doesn't reach you;
My mind is troubled.
Like a toll-keeper at the city gates,
My mind is unhappy.
It cannot become empty
Forgetting the two.
Show me how you can become me,
O Channamallikarjuna, jasmine-tender.

You can become me: the way to complete union.

11

Ever my mind flows to my stomach;
I cannot see your face,
Cannot break your trap of maya.
O Channamallikarjuna, jasmine-tender,
Join me to you, by your grace.

12

To play, to sing, to speak, to ask, to walk, to talk
With your devotees is joyous harmony.
As long as I have
The gift of life from you,
May I spend my days in the company of your devotees,
O Channamallikarjuna, jasmine-tender.

13

What can I know of the initiations, O lord?
I shall remain ever a servant to the servants
Of the wise ones who dedicate themselves
To the guru, the linga and the mendicant,
And thus are freed from egoism.
Therefore I know none
Other than the retinue of
Channamallikarjuna, jasmine-tender.

ayata, svayata: outer and inner initiations, the former with a linga given by the guru, the latter relating it to one's life-breath.

13

14

Even if a hair of his devotee is hurt
Siva will be hurt;
If his devotees change
He too will change.
As scripture proclaims:
'The lord has the body of his devotees' –
Their pain and gain reach Siva.
If the mother is hurt, the baby in the womb is hurt;
Similarly, if his devotees are hurt
Siva himself will be hurt,
See, Channamallikarjuna, jasmine-tender.

15

If the breath itself is fragrant, who needs flowers?
If one has patience, calmness, peace and forbearance
What need is there for the final peace of samadhi?
If one becomes the world itself
What need for solitude
Channamallikarjuna, jasmine-tender?

Samadhi: ultimate peace or illumination, the last of the eight limbs of Yoga, the state which the yogi strives to attain.

16

If you can pull out the fangs
And make it dance,
It is all right to play with the snake.
Free yourself from the bonds of the body;
It is all right to have a body.
Lust is frightening, like one's mother turning into a
     demoness.
Channamallikarjuna, jasmine-tender,
Do not say those you are pleased with
Have taken bodies.

17

The body cannot be without senses,
Nor senses without body;
How can I say I am without desire, without fault?
If you are pleased, I will be happy;
If you are not, I will be sad,
Channamallikarjuna, jasmine-tender.

18

With the two measures of sunrise and sunset,
The grain-heap of life is being measured.
Before it is all over, remember, remember Siva;
This life will not come again.
Remembering Channamallikarjuna, jasmine-tender,
The god of gods,
Even the worst of sinners
Of yore were freed.

19

Within the self of the eight-petalled lotus
Creation was born;
The tortoise swallowed the eight elephants
Which support the universe,
As well as the horizon,
And became real emptiness itself.
Can divisive efforts attain
The true state of self-knowing?
In the sight of my eyes,
In the pleasure of my mind,
I am away from the
Attack of the limbless god of desire.
Can an animal seen in a mirage
Be in the hunter's net?
Men other than my god
Channamallikarjuna, jasmine-tender,
Are not for me (us), O brother.

eight-petalled lotus: consciousness, micro/macrocosmic creation.

the tortoise: one of the ten vital breaths; also the withdrawal of senses from their objects, as when the tortoise withdraws all its limbs into its shell.

eight elephants: depicted as carrying the universe, one in each direction.

emptiness: sunya ('void'), as in Buddhism, is not a vacuum but an absence of specificity.

20

I overcame the trouble of the body
Through the linga,
Overcame the trouble of the mind
Through wisdom,
Overcame the trouble of the separated self
Through the experience of Siva,
Overcame the darkness of the organs
Clothing myself in light.
What your eyes see outside in the glow of youth
Is really the ash of the burnt god of desire, Kama
O Channamallikarjuna, jasmine-tender,
You killed Kama, yet let him
Remain mind-born;
I have wiped out his destiny.

Linga: literally 'sign', the phallic symbol of Siva, indicating procreative power, as well as the ascent of vital energy (see also Introduction).

ash: of the burnt-out triple modalities of nature, the three worlds; worn in three horizontal lines on the forehead and body by devotees of Siva.

Mind-born: one of the names of Kamadeva, the god of desire.

21

Don't insult me, thinking I have no one;
Whatever you do, I won't turn back.
I chew dry leaves,
I lean on an arrowhead.
If Channamallikarjuna, jasmine-tender,
Gives trouble,
Offering the body and breath to you,
I shall become clean.

22

Lord, if you will listen, listen;
If you won't, don't –
I can't bear to live without singing of you.
If you will look, look;
If you won't, don't –
I can't bear life unless I look at you and am happy.
If you will agree, agree;
If you won't, don't –
I can't bear life unless I embrace you.
If you will be pleased, be pleased,
If you won't, don't –
I can't bear life unless I worship you.
O Channamallikarjuna, jasmine-tender,
Offering you worship, I will play
On the swing of happiness.

23

You came with no hesitation, O brother,
As the form was pleasing to your eyes.
You came deluded by a pleasure you heard of,
You came lusting after the female form.
Not seeing that it is only a tube
From which drips piss,
You came, O brother, blinded by desire.
Driving away the supreme meaning by a mind
    perverted,
Not knowing why this is so,
Not realizing this as the supreme source of pain
You came, O brother.
Men other than Channamallikarjuna, jasmine-tender,
Are brothers to me;
Off, get off, you fool.

This as well as the following vacana were addressed to someone who approached Akka with lustful intent.

24

Seeing bare round breasts
And the beauty of full youth
You came, O brother.
Brother, I am no female,
I am not a prostitute;
Then seeing me again and again,
Who did you think I was?
Men other than Channamallikarjuna, jasmine-tender,
Will not suit us, O brother.

25

What if you renounce wealth?
You should not take anything from the senses.
What if you renounce taste?
The tongue-tip should not know sweetness.
What good renouncing woman?
One should be free of desire –
Walking, dreaming and deeply sleeping.
What good is being sky-clad?
The mind should be naked.
Not knowing this fourfold path
They perished in vain,
Channamallikarjuna, jasmine-tender.

Renunciation must come from an inner sufficiency, not just from external restraints.

26

The coward has no happiness, whatever he does.
The brave has no fear, wherever he goes.
The calm has no evil to lower him.
The kind will not be cursed.
One reaching you,
Rid of desire for women and wealth of others,
Has nothing more to fear,
O Channamallikarjuna, jasmine-tender.

27

The warrior won't step back once he enters the field;
For the devotee there is no turning back;
The owner of the mind will delight in the mind.
Few climb the holy mountain;
To climb up and climb down
Is to break the vow.
Entering the arena, if you forget your arms
Channamallikarjuna, jasmine-tender,
The opponent, will pierce and slay you.

28

I went to the forest
Because of the agitation of my body.
I begged of every plant to sustain the body;
They gave me from the bounty of their being.
Begging, I was caught in becoming;
Giving, they become devotees.
I will not beg ever again,
Channamallikarjuna, jasmine-tender, I swear.

See Introduction.

29

What good is a tree, without shade?
What good is wealth, without kindness?
What good is a cow, without milk?
What good is beauty, without grace?
What good is a weapon, without the mind?
What good am I, without knowing you,
Channamallikarjuna, jasmine-tender?

30

Body subdued, mind at rest in you,
To swing in full happiness,
Show me the way.
How can the joy of unchanging emptiness
Come to those who seek it outside?
Channamallikarjuna, jasmine-tender,
Show me the way, to cease to be me
And you remain, O lord.

Wait, wait, O hunger,
Wait, wait, O thirst,
Wait, wait, O sleep,
Wait, wait, O desire,
Wait, wait, O anger,
Wait, wait, O delusion,
Wait, wait, O greed,
Wait, wait, O pride,
Wait, wait, O strife –
All of you, moving and unmoving,
Wait, wait: I am awaiting an urgent summons
From Channamallikarjuna, jasmine-tender.

32

When lightning sparkles
My hunger and thirst are satisfied.
When rain clouds burst over me
I am bathed in holy water.
And if the mountain falls on me,
I will deem it flower offerings.
O Channamallikarjuna, jasmine-tender,
If my head falls off
My life will be an offering to you.

33

The owl blames the sun for its blindness,
The crow blames the moon for its blindness,
The blind blames the mirror for his blindness,
All this is true.
While suffering the hell fires of becoming,
If one says there is no Siva,
No liberation, it is all a lie,
Will Channamallikarjuna, jasmine-tender,
Spare you the suffering of hell?

34

If you cut and grind sandalwood,
Will it stop being fragrant because of the pain?
If you cut and melt gold,
Will it become dirty from the fire?
If you cut sugarcane to pieces and crush it in a mill,
Will it stop being sweet because of the boiling?
If you bring all my past mistakes into view,
Will it harm you, my lord?
I won't leave you, even if you kill me,
O Channamallikarjuna, jasmine-tender.

35

A fisherman, entering water with his net,
Will be happy to catch and kill many creatures.
If a baby dies in his house
He will cry, but never would he cry for all those he
 has killed.
The scripture says,
'One who never discriminates between self and the
 other
But sees all as the light of consciousness, he alone sees.'
The whole world laughs at the crying fisherman.
What shall be said of the carrion-eaters
Who kill and harm beings, even after becoming
 devoted
To Channamallikarjuna, jasmine-tender?

The hell of knowing you itself is emancipation,
Not knowing you, even freedom becomes hell.
Happiness without your grace is sorrow,
Sorrow becomes great happiness by your grace.
O Channamallikarjuna, jasmine-tender,
To me, the chains of your bondage are freedom itself.

37

You build a house on a hill
Yet are frightened of animals;
What then?
You build a house by the sea
And are frightened of the foam and waves;
How would that be?
You build a house in the marketplace
And then are shy of noise;
What would you do?
Listen, O Channamallikarjuna, jasmine-tender.
Once born in the world,
Praised or blamed,
One must not get angry
But remain at peace.

38

What is to come tomorrow,
Let it come to me today.
What is to come today,
Let it come right now.
Do not say then and now,
O Channamallikarjuna, jasmine-tender.

39

You want to see with your eyes,
Yet go into darkness;
How will it be?
To reach the mountain peak
You descend to pits and ravines;
How will it be?
Not satisfied with the alms you give,
I desire other things;
How will it be?
You want to know the greatness of
Channamallikarjuna, jasmine-tender,
Yet are petty;
How will it be?

40

Holding on to the two – true and false –
Goes the whole world.
Holding on to the true and false
Speaks the whole world;
Will the devotee hold on to these two?
The traitor, false to the guru,
The linga and the mendicant,
Lives the worst hell.
All he eats is dirt, all he enjoys is refuse,
All he drinks is inebriating.
Falsehood is the pollutant;
The devotee of Siva knows no falsehood.
If you speak untrue and yet perform worship,
It is like waiting for harvest after sowing chaff,
Is it not, O Channamallikarjuna, jasmine-tender?

See Introduction.

41

Once you have eaten the fruit,
Does it matter who prunes the tree?
Once you have left your woman,
Does it matter who sleeps with her?
Once you have sold your land,
Does it matter who ploughs it?
Once Channamallikarjuna, jasmine-tender,
Is (not) known, does it matter whether
The body is eaten by dogs or rots in water?

See Introduction.

When hungry, a bounty of alms in the villages;
When thirsty, lakes, streams and wells;
To bathe, gurgling springs;
To sleep, temple ruins;
And for a soulmate, I have you,
O Channamallikarjuna, jasmine-tender.

43

What good is the snake swaying
Its head to the tune of the flute
When the poison of desire remains within?
What good is singing and listening
If the baser qualities of self remain?
Show me those who, knowing the inside,
Have forgotten the outside,
O Channamallikarjuna, jasmine-tender.

44

Unless the fruit is ripe
The peel won't come off;
Seeing the insignia of the god of love on the body
Might trouble you, I thought,
So I covered myself.
Why worry about this?
Don't harass one who has entered into
Channamallikarjuna, jasmine-tender,
The God of gods.

🌺

Akka's answer to a question by Allama Prabhu, the mystic
guru-poet of the assembled sages of Kalyana; see Introduction.

45

Like the corpse of an ember,
Like a puppet on a broken string,
Like a lake gone dry,
Like a burnt piece of rope,
Can there be any going back
For one who has found
Refuge in your own body,
O Channamallikarjuna, jasmine-tender?

46

What if the body is dark and scorched?
What if the body is shiny and bright?
What does it matter,
O Channamallikarjuna, jasmine-tender,
How the body you have favoured is,
If the inside is pure?

47

The body was consecrated and offered to you,
The inner organs were offered to you;
I know nothing.
You became my onward path,
You became my mind,
My breath was offered to you.
I won't remember any other than you,
O Channamallikarjuna, jasmine-tender,
I swear.

48

Reading and rereading the Vedas
Led to vain argumentation.
Hearing after hearing of the scriptures
Led to confounding confusion.
Saying I know, I know, the classics
Became hard as rocks.
Saying I have done, have done, the ancient lore
Got lost in wilderness.
Where am I, where is he?
The Absolute is pure space,
O Channamallikarjuna, jasmine-tender.

49

What good is it to us
To eat in someone's house,
To dress in another's house,
And then go guard someone else's door?
What do I care whom you're pleased with?
O Channamallikarjuna, jasmine-tender,
Begging for devotion
My mouth's gone dry.

50

Husband inside, lover outside,
Can't go on with the two.
The worldly and the supreme can't
Be had together.
Can the bow and a wood-apple
Be held together,
Channamallikarjuna, jasmine-tender?

51

She scoops out the head of Kama
And puts out death's eyes.
She roasts, grinds and eats
The sun and the moon;
Who can name her?
You are the bridegroom,
And I the bride,
Like the union of fire and wind
O Channamallikarjuna, jasmine-tender.

52

Wisdom is like the sun
Devotion is like the sunray;
Without the sun the rays cannot be,
Without the rays the sun cannot be.
How can there be
Devotion without wisdom
Or wisdom without devotion,
O Channamallikarjuna, jasmine-tender?

53

One has the here, another the hereafter,
One has no here, another no hereafter.
Another has neither here nor hereafter.
Those who have taken refuge in
Channamallikarjuna, jasmine-tender,
Have both the here and hereafter.

54

Desires were gone, false objects turned back,
Attachment to doubt undone;
Seeing great happiness within,
The mind merged in itself.
By the grace of your sage, Prabhu Deva,
I was saved, O Channamallikarjuna, jasmine-tender.

Prabhu Deva: Allama Prabhu, the mystic-poet guru of the
assembled sages of Kalyana; see Introduction.

55

Show me just once
Those pure in body, mind and heart;
Show me those
Whose every act is the practice of truth
And every word a blessing;
Show me your devotees who,
Having trampled darkness, shine brightly
And remain the same within and without,
Channamallikarjuna, jasmine-tender.

56

I will not say day or night,
Dawn or dusk,
After or before,
I will not say there is any other than you;
Yet the mind does not know greatness, O lord.
Looking in the mirror in the dark
I was troubled,
Without being in light
O Basava, your devotee;
How will I ever see,
O Channamallikarjuna, jasmine-tender?

Basava: founder sage of the Virasaiva movement; see Introduction.

57

I saw the whole, I saw the atom,
I saw the joys of chance,
Of effort and of perception;
Knew knowledge
And forgot forgetfulness.
Wiping out the memory of desire
And knowing you, I became boundless,
O Channamallikarjuna, jasmine-tender.

Most of the terms are used technically in the tradition to refer to different stages of inner transformation. I have tried to render the essence, it being impossible to translate the terms without going into detail beyond the scope of the present translations. Excellent studies on the subject are available.

After the body takes your form,
Whom shall I serve?
After the mind takes your form,
Whom shall I remember?
After the breath takes your form,
Whom shall I worship?
After knowledge has merged in you,
Whom shall I know?
I know you, O Channamallikarjuna, jasmine-tender,
Becoming you in your self.

Total identity with the Absolute, cancelling out all differences,
is indicated.

59

All the Vedas, scriptures and
Sacred lore, canons and codes
Are but grist and husk ground in the mill.
Why grind this, why winnow?
When you behead the mind that
Flows here and there,
O Channamallikarjuna, jasmine-tender,
There remains eternal space.

Vedas, scriptures, etc.: veda, sastra, purana, agama all refer to obligatory ritualistic injunctions, the 'heard it said' part of scriptures, which is transcended in the direct experience of their meaning.

60

Can you have one husband for the here,
And another for the hereafter?
Can you have one husband for the mundane,
Another for the ultimate?
All husbands other than my
Channamallikarjuna, jasmine-tender,
Are like puppets hidden by clouds.

❧

here, hereafter: translations of iha and para; see note to 53.
mundane: laukika, literally 'worldly'.

61

What is full won't spill,
What has trust won't doubt,
What has come together won't part,
What is wholly known won't be forgotten.
O Channamallikarjuna, jasmine-tender,
The devotee in whom you are well pleased
Will have boundless joy.

62

I am pleased with you, you are pleased with me;
You do not stray away from me,
I do not stray away from you;
For you and me, is there another space?
I know that you are all mercy;
I stay where you have put me.
You know all this, don't you,
O Channamallikarjuna, jasmine-tender?

63

I am united with the beautiful one who has
No death, no fault, no form.
O mother, I am united with the
Handsome one who has
No end, no break, no compare, no distinguishing mark,
No birth, no fear.
Brave is he, the beautiful one I am joined to;
I am united with the boundlessly expansive
Channamallikarjuna, jasmine-tender.
All these husbands who die and decay –
Throw them in the fire, mother.

64

I touch the feet of Kama once,
Then again, beseech the moon with folded palms:
This separation be damned.
Why must I be perturbed?
Because of Channamallikarjuna, jasmine-tender,
I am obliged to everyone.

65

The sorrowful mind turned upside down,
The cool breeze turned fiery,
The full moon became hot.
Like a toll collector at the city gates
My mind strayed.
Pacify him and bring him back, O mother;
Channamallikarjuna, jasmine-tender,
has the anger of two.

66

I burned in a fire that had no fuel, O mother,
Suffered from a wound not open.
I wandered seeking happiness, O mother;
In love with Channamallikarjuna, jasmine-tender,
I lived through ordeals that should not have been.

67

For the mind to see its own logic,
And to experience itself, is possible only if
The memory is expansive.
How can it be stopped
By rules of reason?
O mother, you are a fool.
Pleased as I am with my
Channamallikarjuna, jasmine-tender,
I am wholly his.
I won't agree
To your maternal claims; go away.

68

If I hide in a stone, you become the stone;
If I burrow into hill, you become the hill.
O samsara, you come climbing on
One back after another.
O Channamallikarjuna, jasmine-tender,
What now, now what?

Samsara: the phenomenon of becoming, cyclic repetition of birth and death; the opposite of nirvana, 'liberation'.

69

The fiery world of becoming
Follow and trouble me, without respite,
Whatever shall I do?
What shall I do for the sufferings
That come daily, O lord?
What use in carrying around
The burden of this burned body?
O Channamallikarjuna, jasmine-tender,
Slay me or save me; you decide.

becoming: see note to 68.

70

The hateful samsara is my father.
My tribe is looking for me:
They hunt me down
And are killing me.
I have come to you for refuge;
Protect me, hear my cry,
O Channamallikarjuna, jasmine-tender.

71

The truth of the body was lost,
Dispassion of the mind undone;
Sorrow blinds, I cannot see the glory.
Even the wise old ones are perplexed.
This veil of becoming
That hides you won't let me near,
O Channamallikarjuna, jasmine-tender.

72

When I was born, samsara was born;
When samsara was born, ignorance was born;
When ignorance was born, desire was born;
When desire was born, anger was born.
Blinded by the inert smoke of that fire of anger,
I forgot you and
Became prey to pains of the world.
Remove my forgetfulness, take me and
Make known your feet,
O Channamallikarjuna, jasmine-tender.

Samsara ('becoming'), with its chains starting with ignorance,
desire, anger (frustration), loss of memory, etc., belongs to the
wisdom discourse of Indian psychology. See *Bhagavadgita*
chapter 2, verses 62–63.

73

Look at this woman who,
Entering the fireplace,
Has forgotten the fire;
Going up the mountain,
Has forgotten the tumult.
See this attachment to samsara:
This will not leave one for lives numerous.
Waistbelt fastened or no waistbelt
Is the same to me.
What will you look for in me,
O Channamallikarjuna, jasmine-tender?

74

O, alas, the vanity of samsara
Came and played havoc.
With the mask of the father
It came at the beginning.
With the mask of a handsome youth
With waxed moustache,
It played in the middle.
With the mask of senile old age
It played at the end.
If your seeing stops,
The dance of the universe also stops,
O Channamallikarjuna, jasmine-tender.

75

What have I to do with this
Dying puppet of the world,
A dirty bundle of illusion,
A castle of sorrow?
What do I care for
A broken water pot, which drips?
The finger can only touch,
Not eat the fruit.
Consciousness is life;
I am not worried seeing this.
Accept my faults,
O Channamallikarjuna, jasmine-tender.

Some sources have the second part of the first two lines as
'I am the puppet...' But the rest of the vacana agrees better
with the sense (as in the source I have used) of Akka's strong
disengagement from the body.

76

For his pleasure he created the universe,
For his pleasure he wove into it this world,
For his own pleasure, he made it go round in endless
Suffering of cyclic becoming.
When Channamallikarjuna, jasmine-tender,
The supreme Siva,
Has had enough of this phenomenal dance,
He will sever the bonds of illusion.

illusion: maya.

77

Born in lives that
Should not have been,
Burning in sorrows unending,
I have now stumbled upon
The path of your mercy.
To become one in body,
Mind merged in my god
Channamallikarjuna, jasmine-tender,
To be deep love,
Where there is no other,
When will it be, O father?

78

He makes you take birth in wombs unborn,
Makes you suffer untold miseries,
Makes you eat what is not eaten,
And traps you in fate, O brother.
Will he spare you
Because you say you are his own?
He tore the skin off Bhrungi, his attendant;
Will he be mindful of others?
Channamallikarjuna, jasmine-tender,
Is vicious,
So don't let go of him.

Bhrungi: a skeleton form of Andhaka the blind, one of Siva's attendants.

79

Like the silk worm weaving its home
In love, out of its own body,
And dying in its own strangling threads,
Mind's desires unending
Set me on fire;
Rid my mind of greed,
Draw me near,
O Channamallikarjuna, jasmine-tender.

In love: sneha ('oil') can also mean 'love'.

Pot of refuse,
Vessel of piss,
Mat of bones,
Stench of pus –
Burn this body.
Don't be destroyed
Holding on to the body;
Know Channamallikarjuna, jasmine-tender,
You fool.

81

Not one, not two, not three, not four,
But eighty-four hundred thousand are the wombs
I have come through.
Made to be what I couldn't be,
I ate joys and sorrows.
Let the life of the past be;
Please show your kindness hereafter,
Channamallikarjuna, jasmine-tender.

eighty-four hundred thousand: the number of births in different life forms, from the ant to the human, according to popular belief. Akka here dismisses them all in a prospective supplication/vision.

82

Don't be destroyed, don't be destroyed,
Hold fast to the feet of Siva.
This body of yours is not indestructible,
The pleasures of the world do not last forever.
Before the word that Channamallikarjuna, jasmine-
    tender,
Wrote is wiped off,
Take refuge in Siva, soon.

The word (etc.): the initiatory mantra namassivaya.

83

Like a worm I writhed in pain;
Like grains of sand, I was scattered;
Sorrowful even in dreams, I trembled.
I was steamed to pulp as in a pot,
No friend to share my troubles.
Grant me your grace
So that I get a body
Better than the one I sought,
And happiness that
Cannot be added to,
O Channamallikarjuna, jasmine-tender.

84

Listen to my request,
Accept my request,
Grant my request.
Why won't you listen
To my wailing,
O father?
There is none other than you, none,
You are my onward path,
You, my mind,
O Channamallikarjuna, jasmine-tender.

85

As an elephant
Separated from its herd
And trapped remembers his Vindhyan forests,
I remember you.
As a bird in a cage
Remembers its mate,
I remember you.
Say 'Come here, my son'
And show your true form,
O Channamallikarjuna, jasmine-tender.

86

As the sun is seed to
The movements of the world,
The mind is seed to
The movement of the senses.
I have but one mind;
If it gets merged in you,
What sorrow have I,
O Channamallikarjuna, jasmine-tender?

87

I was trapped in samsara;
The guru showed me that samsara was empty.
Checking the attachment to body forms,
The guru placed the mark of the lord on my body;
He wiped away my past,
And led me onward.
My guru revealed the truth of
Channamallikarjuna, jasmine-tender.

Guru: literally 'that which dispels darkness'; see Introduction.
Body forms, mark of the lord: translations of anga and linga respectively.

88

Before earth joins earth,
Before water joins water,
Before fire joins fire,
Before air joins air,
Before space joins space,
Before the five senses wear out,
Take refuge in
Channamallikarjuna, jasmine-tender.

earth joins earth (etc.): final dissolution of the created elements
into their pre-created, pure states.

89

Clarifying the inside, purifying the outside,
Removing the doubt of within–without,
Causing to shine like crystal:
Like sowing suitable seed in a good field,
Bringing the phenomenal conditionings
Of the disciple to a stop,
Instructing him in truth,
And leading him on the path of truth,
Dwells the wisdom teacher.
He is to be adored by the whole universe.
I bow to his holy feet again and again.
O Channamallikarjuna, jasmine-tender.

Wisdom teacher: the guru.

90

When the true guru blessing the disciple
Touches his forehead,
It is like the philosopher's stone
Falling on metal.
If the guru smears holy ashes on his forehead,
He is anointed
Sovereign of the state of liberation.
The five vessels representing
The faces of the creator overflowed
With the nectar of the Siva's Grace,
Like gushing springs.
Amidst assembled devotees,
The great mark of the lord
Was placed in the disciple's hand,
Like a gooseberry in the palm.
The initiatory chant
Spoken in the ear and bracelet tied,
The body became the abode of Siva,
The vital breath became the linga
Made up of the five Brahmas.
I was saved by the guru's presence
That showed me the way onward,
Liberating me from the past,
O Channamallikarjuna, jasmine-tender.

true guru: sadguru, a guru established in the real, existential truth, to be understood in the context of the transmission of wisdom to a satsishya, or earnest student-disciple. The rest of the vacana refers to different stages of the disciple's initiation.

91

As you remain
Like water in milk,
I do not know
What is behind, what ahead;
I do not know
Who is master, who servant;
I do not know
What is great, what small.
With your grace,
Will not a mere ant become Rudra, the terrible?
O Channamallikarjuna, jasmine-tender?

Rudra: the 'Wild God', the primordial being who split into man
and woman, a name of Siva; the vacana refers to the initiation
sequence in the Siva tradition.

92

O Guru, who protects
Those who seek refuge,
Hail! Victory to you.
You grasped the space within space
That no one knows
And handed it to me,
O Guru Channamallikarjuna, jasmine-tender,
Hail! Victory to you.

This vacana again refers to the initiation and empowerment of the guru–sishya dialectics as understood in the perpetual transmission of wisdom.

Space within space: the point of origination as well as culmination; also called 'space of the heart'.

93

The eternal walked into my house today;
Liberation walked into my house today;
Hail! O auspicious one,
Adorations, O Guru,
Adorations, O Supreme Guru.
O Guru, who showed me
Channamallikarjuna, jasmine-tender,
Hail!

94

Like a river in spate
Flooding a parched lake,
Like rain drenching a drying plant,
Today, it is as if the joys of this world
And the path beyond
Came to me, walking hand in hand.
O Channamallikarjuna, jasmine-tender,
Seeing the guru's feet
I am fulfilled.

This world and beyond: iha, 'here', and para, 'beyond'; see
note to 53.

95

The guru was the mediator,
The linga the bridegroom,
I was the bride.
Let the whole world know
The countless devotees are my parents,
I was given in marriage
To one fully matching.
So, Channamallikarjuna, jasmine-tender,
Himself is my husband;
I have nothing to do
With the rest of the world, O lord.

Mediator: tettiga, literally 'kinsman'; sometimes translated as 'priest'. Traditionally, marriages are arranged, usually by a close relative.

Fully matching: literally 'looking alike'; denotes total compatibility.

96

With a floor of emeralds,
Festoons of gold and diamond pillars,
A roof of coral,
Pearls and jewels for ceiling,
I was married;
My people had me married.
With bracelets and amulets
And everlasting food stock,
I was given in marriage to
Channamallikarjuna, jasmine-tender.

The whole vacana has esoteric meaning in Siva-Yoga practice.
The 'mystical marriage' is known also in other traditions.

The water from washing the guru's feet
Is a holy bath for me,
Sacred ashes are turmeric
For my face,
The quarters of space my wedding dress,
The dust off the feet of Siva's devotees, unguent,
Rudraksha beads my jewellery;
The sandals of devotees
Are the jewel-combs for my hair.
I am the bride of Channamallikarjuna, jasmine-tender;
What need have I
Of other decorations, O mother?

Traditional practice in the guru-disciple context; Jesus washing
the disciple's feet also belongs to this universal tradition, and
shows the interchangeability of counterparts.

Rudraksha beads: sacred to Siva, worn by his followers; also
medicinal.

98

I burned in an endless fire of longing
To have you for my husband, O Siva.
When there was talk of nuptial bed,
My people sent me to the crescent-wearing Siva,
They covered me with ashes and tied bracelets;
Channamallikarjuna, jasmine-tender,
Made me his own.

Supposedly Akka's response to Allama Prabhu when he
questioned her on arrival at the 'auspicious assembly' of
devotees; see Introduction.

Crescent-wearing: the thin crescent adorning Siva's head
represents the mind, sublimated to its purest functioning.

99

Over a bower of water,
A roof of fire,
Hailstones spread as a nuptial bed,
Festoons of flowers –
A legless woman married a headless man;
I was given over to life eternal.
Channamallikarjuna, jasmine-tender,
Married me, O mother.

A vacana that refers to the mystical union of the mind with the
Absolute.

100

By the guru's grace I saw the linga,
I saw the mendicant.
By the guru's grace I saw
The holy water from rinsing his feet,
I saw the gift of grace.
By the guru's grace,
I saw the blessed ways of
The truly devout.
O Channamallikarjuna, jasmine-tender,
As soon as I was born
The guru put the insignia of holy ashes
And made me belong to the linga,
And thus I was fulfilled.

101

I adore the guru who,
Removing the human birth,
Transformed it to a divine one.
I adore the guru who,
Undoing the bonds of becoming,
Showed me supreme bliss.
I adore the guru who,
Changing me from being sorrowful,
Made me a devotee.
I adore the guru who
Gave me custody of
Channamallikarjuna, jasmine-tender.

102

Hell here – this side,
The holy feet there – afar,
The ten directions of space here – this side,
The ten hands there – afar.
The expanding universe here – this side,
The jewelled crown there – afar.
O Channamallikarjuna, jasmine-tender,
You are well set in my palm.

103

The guru gave a symbol
Lest I forget;
If you know, the real symbol is different,
O brother.
Why worry about uncertain devotion?
If you know and worship
Channamallikarjuna, jasmine-tender,
Will you return to this world of pain?

Symbol: literally 'symbol' in the first line; in the third, it is prana-linga, the vital-breath linga, here translated as the 'real-symbol'.

104

Like a good girl I will bathe you;
Calmly I will worship;
In harmonious love, I will sing your praise.
O Channamallikarjuna, jasmine-tender,
I can now worship
Without straying from you.

A vacana that refers to the ritual practices of the worship of the Siva-linga.

105

Worshipping the linga in hand,
I waved bright camphor lights.
The sight of the eyes,
The hardened thoughts,
Unfulfilled desire –
I knew no way, O lord.
Now I can worship you,
Channamallikarjuna, jasmine-tender,
Without going away from you.

The linga in hand: the Virasaiva initiates worship a miniature linga given by the guru, called the ishta-linga. This is the 'symbol' referred to in the preceding verses.

106

If you say you know,
It cannot be known.
The great alone is great;
Not fully knowing
Channamallikarjuna, jasmine-tender,
You have failed.

You have failed: the vacana does not make clear who failed; it could be you, I or s/he!

What is good
For all people of the world is there:
Religion, scriptures, epics and
Revealed texts.
There is the path of devotion
And the rising of the light.
If you wear ashes, becoming stops,
The aggregates of suffering vanish,
And one comes close, in the world of Siva,
And gains identity with him.
Have faith, this ash frightens births away.
The sages Agastya, Kasyapa and Jamadagni
Wore this to be free from the fear of death.
This ash pleases well
Channamallikarjuna, jasmine-tender,
The lord of the mountain.

If ... ashes: ashes stand for the pure residue left after all else is burnt out in the fire of wisdom.

Agastya: a sage associated with the south, especially with the ancient Tamil culture and language; reputed to have drunk the ocean dry when the demons were hiding there in their battle with the gods.

Kasyapa: a sage, son of Brahma, and a prajapati (lord of creation); also the priest of Rama.

Jamadagni: a sage of the line of Bhrugu; the father of Parasurama and husband of Renuka.

108

Seventy million great mantras;
Secondary chants are countless;
Do not be confused
With all the sorrow, O mind!
'Adorations again and again, O Siva';
Saying thus if one takes refuge
Is it not enough?
If asked how,
It is said:
'Even ten million great sins
Are burnt to ashes
If one recites the name of Siva.'
Thus, for me, this is the mantra
This is the tantra,
This alone my way, mind and life.
This is my supreme philosophy:
It showed me the real guru,
Channamallikarjuna, jasmine-tender.

Direct bipolar relationship (as opposed to elaborate injunctions and prohibitions regarding his worship) to the Absolute, Siva, is recommended in this vacana.

'Even ten million ... Siva': a quotation from the Sanskrit *Ashtavaranastotram*, 'hymn in praise of the eight veils'.

Mantra, tantra, yantra: terms used in Tantrism; yantra is a geometric design, perceptual form, mantra the word or alphabet, the algebraic, conceptual name, while tantra is the technique or know-how of putting the two together.

109

The frog in the snake's mouth leaps for the fly –
The seeking of nourishment never stops;
See the lie that the body is surrendered,
See this shame that I am devoted,
See this disgusting pride that I am united.
No more food offerings, no gifts of grace,
O Channamallikarjuna, jasmine-tender,
Till the two merge.

Food-offering ... grace: traditionally part of the ritual of worship.

Till the two merge: literally 'both' merge or subside. The total elimination of the distinction between 'worshipped' and 'worshipper' is indicated.

110

As long as one heaps up good and bad,
It is only a body of desire,
A knowledge of hate,
A being of covetousness,
An abode of delusion,
A veil of vanity,
A cover of competitive greed.
Till such being is cut off
There is no room to know
Channamallikarjuna, jasmine-tender.

Good and bad: the need to transcend the duality, rather than simply being 'good' in a one-sided sense, is stressed.

Desire … greed: a reference to the six well-known 'enemies' in Indian contemplative traditions.

111

I am full of desire for action,
Full of desire to be among your devotees;
If I climb the holy mountain
And mix with you,
Will my desires end, O Lord?
I came without any desire,
Full of faith in you,
And perished,
O Channamallikarjuna, jasmine-tender.

112

Actions won't reach you;
How will I worship you?
Sounds won't reach you;
How will I sing of you?
If the body reaches,
You are invisible greatness;
How shall I wear you in my palm?
Not knowing anything of myself,
Looking at you again and again
I am amazed,
O Channamallikarjuna, jasmine-tender.

Sounds: nadabindu in the original denotes the creative logos,
sound and the beginning point of space, a point of origination
or culmination.

113

Like the monkey at the tip of a pole,
Like the puppet at the end of a string,
I played as you made me play,
I spoke as you made me speak,
I stayed as you made me stay:
Till Channamallikarjuna, jasmine-tender,
The machinist of the world,
Said 'Enough'.

Machinist: literally 'machine bearer', meaning technician, engineer, director.

114

Disgusted with becoming,
The mind has embraced death.
What shall I do, O lord?
Laden with sorrow,
The mind turned upside down,
What shall I do, O lord?
To be in a state of non-separation,
To melt and merge in you but once,
To be in your state of eternal joy,
When will it be,
O Channamallikarjuna, jasmine-tender?

115

Don't trust him
For his coaxing ways;
He is a cheat, this knower of the world.
Showing liberation,
He makes you forget devotion,
Channamallikarjuna, jasmine-tender.

Knower of the world: vijnani, one who knows the specific applications of wisdom.

Liberation, devotion: literal translations of mukti and bhakti.

116

Like a statue listening
To the recital of a wax parrot,
The one reciting has no life,
The listener has no knowledge;
The devotion of one
Who does not know you
Is like the statue listening
To the recital of the wax parrot,
O Channamallikarjuna, jasmine-tender.

117

Will those who are harmoniously joined in love
Inquire after family and tribe?
Will unconscious folk feel shame?
What will those who have joined
Channamallikarjuna, jasmine-tender,
Know of the ways of the world?

118

The servant must offer the master the best thing;
This is the difference between master and servant.
If devoted to the linga,
One must wash the feet of the mendicant,
Offer this water to the linga,
And only then should one eat;
This is the secret, this is the dharma,
O Channamallikarjuna, jasmine-tender.

Servant, master: dialectical equating of counterparts.

Linga, mendicant: see Introduction.

Dharma: used here to mean correct behaviour, but usually refers to general religious or spiritual duty, or to natural law.

119

Beyond compare are the devotees of the lord;
They are my kith and kin.
If our lord of the holy mountain,
Channamallikarjuna, jasmine-tender,
Is pleased with me,
I won't come this way again,
O mother.

Devotees: a simpler rendering of 'hosts of Rudra'.
Holy mountain: srisaila, one of the famous temples, where Siva is worshipped as Channamallikarjuna.

120

Troubled by the five senses,
A potful of pride,
The youthful body has gone in vain, alas!
As the bumblebee, drinking
Fragrance, stops fluttering –
When will you take me in,
O Channamallikarjuna, jasmine-tender.

Bumblebee: used to describe the mind attaining a state of bliss
whose source is within the self, and thus ceasing to wander.

121

Life slips away,
Future is going to ruin;
Beloved wife and children
Go their own ways.
Do not die barren, O mind, don't:
In the company of devotees of
Channamallikarjuna, jasmine-tender,
I found secure life, O mind.

122

Four quarters of the day
They rush for food;
Four quarters of the night
They rush to sorrow.
Like the washerman who stands in water
Yet dies of thirst,
They know not the great treasure
That is in themselves,
O Channamallikarjuna, jasmine-tender.

123

We have thoughts of the linga,
We have thoughts of our devotees,
We have thoughts of our first ones.
Other than the thought of our
Channamallikarjuna, jasmine-tender,
Why do we want
To talk of the world, O brother?

Devotees, first ones: refer to the devotees at various levels of perfection in their devotion.

124

The courtyard of the Siva devotee
Is Varanasi, is it not true?
In his courtyard the sixty-eight
Holy springs, is it not so?
The scriptures bear witness:
'If one drinks the waters of Kedar
Or dies at Varanasi
Or looks at the holy mountain,
One shall not be born again.'
If you turn around,
To the left and right is Kedar
And just outside is Varanasi.
With dispassion for seed
And devotion for sprout,
O Channamallikarjuna, jasmine-tender,
Your devotees' courtyard
Is a grain greater than the holy confluence.

Varanasi: Banaras, Kasi.
Kedar: Kedarnath in the Himalayas, a place of pilgrimage
sacred to Siva.

125

By the words of the joyful,
Sorrow got a respite;
When emotion was intimate,
Memory got a respite.
By associating with your devotees
I became merged in you
And your love contained me,
O Channamallikarjuna, jasmine-tender.

126

If you look, speak and listen,
It is a great joy.
What is impossible with
The grace of your devotees?
O Channamallikarjuna, jasmine-tender,
To the assemblage of your devotees
What is impossible?

127

Associating with the ignorant
Is like trying to light a fire
By rubbing stones;
Associating with the wise
Is like taking butter
After churning curd.
O Channamallikarjuna, jasmine-tender,
Associating with your devotees
Is like a hill of camphor
Catching fire.

Camphor catching fire: camphor leaves no residue after burning.

128

Why do you make me talk?
My hair is loose, my face is sad,
My body is melting.
O brothers, why do you make me talk?
O fathers, I have been through much,
Becoming has stopped for me,
Crooked ways are no more.
Becoming devoted, I have joined
Channamallikarjuna, jasmine-tender,
And am free of family.

A vacana that addresses the assembly of devotees at Kalyana.

129

Show me those who have forgotten
The changing ways of the senses
And have joined themselves to the linga.
Show me those who,
Having loosened the bonds
Of the darkness of lust,
Have devotion for life-breath.
Show me the true devotees,
Pure in body, mind and speech,
Who have taken refuge in your grace,
O Channamallikarjuna, jasmine-tender.

130

I suffered meditating on sorrow,
Can't see the linga of light.
He won't be caught in strings of words;
He withers the marrow, troubles the mind.
If one knows the supreme
As well as oneself
He is the yogi.
I bow to his feet,
O Channamallikarjuna, jasmine-tender.

131

Does not a chain bind,
Be it made of gems?
Does not a net restrain,
Be it made of pearls?
If heads are cut off
With a golden knife,
Will they not die?
If caught in devotion
To the dividing ways of the world
Will birth and death cease,
O Channamallikarjuna, jasmine-tender?

132

For the coming of your devotees, O lord,
I will decorate the temple with festoons.
For the coming of your devotees, O lord,
I will wear my royal headgear,
O lord, if your devotees come to my house,
I will plant their lotus feet in my heart,
See, Channamallikarjuna, jasmine-tender.

133

O lord, having seen your true devotees,
The veil over my eyes was torn off today;
Having bowed at the holy feet of your true devotees,
The fate written over my forehead was wiped off today.
O Channamallikarjuna, jasmine-tender,
Having seen the feet of Basavanna, your devotee,
I kept bowing in adoration, again and again.

134

I defeated Kama, the god of desire,
O Basava, by your strength.
By your grace, O Basava,
I will hold on to the moon-wearer.
What if I am called by a woman's name?
In meditation, my form is masculine,
O Basava, by your kindness.
Restraining the over-lustful
Channamallikarjuna, jasmine-tender,
I am united, not knowing the two,
O Basava, by your mercy?

A vacana in praise of Basava, the founder leader of the assembly of devotees.

Moon-wearer: Siva; see note to 98.

Masculine: here stands for strength (of purpose).

Over-lustful: Siva is ever impatient for union with the devotee.

Desiring, imagining, I sat, O mother, being scorched;
Deluded kissing, I went mad, O mother;
Ever, never giving up, I believed him with joy.
If my god, Channamallikarjuna, jasmine-tender,
Does not like me
What shall I do, O mother?

136

Listen, my friend, listen. I had a dream:
I saw a mendicant, seated on the hill;
This beggar with red matted locks and pearly teeth
    came and loved me.
Embracing him, I was afraid.
Seeing the jasmine-tender Channamallikarjuna,
I closed and opened my eyes, wonder-struck.

One of a number of vacanas that describe Akka's dream of
uniting with her beloved lord, sometimes with slight variations.
Siva as the handsome beggar, irresistibly attractive, is found
also in the puranas (ancient lore, legends).

Opened my eyes: some texts have 'closed and opened my eyes';
opening to the inner vision and withdrawal from the outward-
directed senses indicated.

137

I have worn turmeric paste over my body,
Ornaments of gold,
And clothes fit for gods.
Come, O man,
Come, O jewel among men:
Your coming is the coming of my own life breath.
Come, O jasmine-tender Channamallikarjuna,
Waiting for your coming
My mouth is all dry.

Turmeric paste: used as an antiseptic and as a beauty aid by women in India.

Gold, clothes fit for gods: all symbols of great value, corresponding to the value of the adored 'jewel among men'.

Waiting: literally 'watching the path'.

138

Seeing the divine form
That shines in splendour
Within the eyes, I forgot myself, O mother.
Seeing the beauty of the jewelled crown, the snake
    bracelet,
Smiling face, and the pearly teeth,
My mind vanished.
So, Channamallikarjuna, jasmine-tender,
Is my bridegroom
And I his bride; listen, O mother.

139

O lord, what shall I say of the ways
Of the wise ones, born from the linga?
Their ways are the scriptures,
Their speech is the Vedas;
Can they be said to belong to the world?
For this scripture bears witness:
'As the seed born of the tree,
Again gets merged in the tree,
Those who leave the world of Rudra
Are born in the world of Siva.'
From the seed the mighty fig tree is born,
That tree again inheres in the seed;
Similarly, from the linga
The wise ones are born,
Then they merge again in the linga.
Taking refuge in these wise ones
I am free from birth,
See, Channamallikarjuna, jasmine-tender.

140

Over his red, radiant matted locks
Shines the tender white crescent.
He wears snake jewels for earrings,
And a garland of skulls.
If you see him, O mother,
Ask him to come just once.
The eye of Govinda is on his toe;
This is how you can recognize
Channamallikarjuna, jasmine-tender.

141

I saw the divine form
With shining red matted hair for diadem,
Pleasing rows of shining pearly teeth
And smiling face;
Illuminating the twice-seven worlds
With the glow of his eyes.
Seeing him, my eyes' famine
Is gone today.
I saw the great one
Who makes all the males female.
I saw the supreme guru
Channamallikarjuna, jasmine-tender,
Ever united with the primal Sakti.
Seeing him, I am saved.

Twice-seven worlds: according to popular belief there are fourteen worlds, seven in ascending and seven in descending order, with the earth being placed in the middle; different scales of values are implied.

Makes all the males females: a notion found in mystical traditions throughout the world.

Primal Sakti: the positive as well as negative aspects of the Absolute, being and becoming.

142

Listen, O sister, I had a dream:
I saw rice, betel nut, coconut
And palm leaf festoons;
I saw the mendicant with small matted locks
And shining pearly teeth,
Come begging, O sister.
I ran after him and caught him by the hand
While he was running away;
Seeing Channamallikarjuna, jasmine-tender,
I opened my eyes.

A vacana in which the dream theme recurs.

Rice, betel nut, etc.: symbols of abundance, used as decorations at all auspicious occasions, especially marriages.

Opened my eyes: arrived at true understanding.

143

O birds that keep on chattering,
Have you seen, have you seen?
O swans that play in the great lakes,
Have you seen, have you seen?
O cuckoos that sing in high notes,
Have you seen, have you seen?
O bumblebees that swarm and play around,
Have you seen, have you seen?
O peacocks that dance on mountain peaks,
Have you seen, have you seen?
If you know, please do tell me
Where Channamallikarjuna, jasmine-tender, is.

144

O bumblebees, O great tree,
O lustrous moon, O koel bird,
I beg just one thing from each of you:
If you see my lord,
Channamallikarjuna, jasmine-tender,
Please call and show me.

145

If the cloth that covers them slips,
Men and women become shy.
If you, lord of life,
Envelop the whole world,
What is there to be shy of?
If Channamallikarjuna, jasmine-tender,
Sees with the whole world as eyes,
What shall you cover and hide, O man?

146

I went watching the path of the stars
In the boundless ocean of glory
Shipping things from island to island.
If I know the silent speech of
Channamallikarjuna, jasmine-tender,
He will take me, as before.

Reference is made in the vacana to yogic practices: the islands
may be the cakras, and the silent speech the ultimate silence
in union.

As before: before the separation.

147

Kama, the god of desire, does not know;
He was burnt to ashes.
Time, who is death, does not know;
He was trampled down.
Brahma, the creator, does not know;
His head was plucked off.
Listen, O mother, listen:
Vishnu, the preserver, does not know;
He had to tend cattle.
The three worlds do not know;
They were burned by the eye in the forehead.
Therefore, Channamallikarjuna, jasmine-tender, is
    my husband,
What shall I describe of his greatness,
Beyond birth and death,
O mother?

The vacana contains references to the various gods being punished for their non-absolutist positions in regard to understanding the Supreme, here called Siva; all references are to popular mythology as found in the puranas.

Time ... death: the god of death, also Time as the All-devouring Kala.

148

Within the body, the bodiless came to be;
Within the individuated,
The non-individuated came to be;
Within becoming, the becomingless came to be;
Within the mind, great remembrance came to be;
O Channamallikarjuna, jasmine-tender,
As you have nurtured me,
Seeing to my head, breasts and such organs,
I belong to your true way.

Seeing to … organs: perhaps meaning that, while these organs belong to Nature, as a woman the poet is troubled by their ability to arouse passion in men.

149

Beyond the body, beyond the mind,
Beyond the great,
Beyond that there is no logic,
As there is no thinker;
Channamallikarjuna, jasmine-tender,
Is the real principle, unreachable.

The great: ghana, 'weighty', and maha, 'great', found in different texts, refer to the causal factor from which the mind arises.

Logic: tarkane is usually translated 'witness' but can also be 'logic', from tarka, a branch of Indian logic, nyaya. The usual ratiocinative methods are not enough to reach the Absolute.

Unreachable: some readings have 'the principle that cannot merge with Channamallikarjuna', but the text adopted here makes more sense, Channamallikarjuna himself being the principle.

150

Trees rubbing against each other
Fired sparks that burned the trees around.
Minds rubbing against each other
Understanding was born,
And it burned the enveloping bodily qualities;
Show me such wisdom of the wise
And save me,
Channamallikarjuna, jasmine-tender.

Minds: originally mana mana, 'mind and mind'.

151

Make me go from house to house
Begging with outstretched palms, O lord!
Even if I beg, O lord,
See that they don't give.
If they give, O lord,
Make it fall to the ground.
When it falls to the ground, O lord,
See that the dog gets it before I pick it up,
Channamallikarjuna, jasmine-tender.

The renunciant is enjoined by the tradition to beg for bodily sustenance, like a honeybee, so that s/he can devote all effort to learning and teaching.

152

The hunger for food, the thirst for drink,
The wild fire of sorrow, the agitation of sense-bonds,
The delusions of three kinds of suffering, I've
    overcome.
What else, O, what more do I need!
I won't turn away from you,
O Channamallikarjuna, jasmine-tender, I will not.

❧

The three kinds of suffering: psychological, cosmological and
theological.

153

Not if you wander, searching, not even if you keep
    vows,
Not if you beg in longing, not if you burn in penance,
It will not happen unless it's the right time,
It won't be attained till Siva is pleased;
As Channamallikarjuna, jasmine-tender, is pleased
    with me,
I saw the holy feet of Basava of the confluence,
I am saved.

The divine factor/Chance/Time has an important role in the
fruition of the search, missed by egoistic, one-sided effort.
Surrendering to/serving gurus and the following of their path
is indicated by the reference to the 'holy feet of Basava'.

Basava of the confluence: Kudalasangama, the confluence of
the Krishna and Malaprabha rivers; an important centre of
pilgrimage for the poet-saint Basava.

154

Even if I want to stay apart,
Your maya will not leave me;
Even if I struggle against it, this maya stays unbroken;
Your maya doesn't leave even if one stands firm;
Those striving to break this maya
Are themselves broken.
To the yogi, your maya became the yogini;
To the ascetic, maya was the fair woman ascetic.
For the god, the assumption of monthly
Offerings was the illusion;
If one climbed the mountain, maya,
Restless, climbed after.
If one walks deep into the forest, maya goes along;
O samsara, it does not leave my back, my hands;
It gives me faith and then makes me forget.
O mercy maker, I am afraid of your maya,
O supreme master, Channamallikarjuna, jasmine-
    tender,
Have mercy.
What else, O what shall I do, O great god.
O snake-adorned one, do have mercy, O god.

A vacana found only in the edition compiled by Dr L. Basavaraju
(Mysore: Geetha Publishing House, 1995).

155

O god, when will I be rid of attachment to the
    worldly one, O father?
When will I be able to delight in true devotion,
    unmixed, my father?
When will you release my mind
Which does not really merge in its devotions, O lord?
When will you pluck out my eyes
Fixed (on others), my lord
Channamallikarjuna, jasmine-tender?

A vacana from the edition cited on page 154.

Eyes fixed (on others): literally 'eyes fixed in the worship'; may mean caught up in the external ritualistic show as opposed to true worship, becoming one with the object of worship.

156

How to please you, O lord, with the eight-fold
offerings?
You are beyond all external transactions.
How to please you with meditating in inner space?
You are beyond word and mind.
How to please you with chants and praises?
You are beyond sound.
How to please you with the knowledge of your
becoming?
You are beyond the intellect.
How to please you by placing my love in the middle
of the heart-lotus?
You fill every part.
It is not for me to please you, O lord;
Your grace is well-being.
O Channamallikarjuna, jasmine-tender.

The eight-fold offerings: performed with the following articles
of worship: unbroken rice, sandal paste, water, betel leaf,
waving of lights, incense, bilva leaves and food. Siva is
beyond the reach of such materialistic forms of worship.

157

Climbing the sapphire hill,
Clasping the moonstone image close,
Blowing the antler horn, when will I get to sit, O Siva?
The brokenness of the body and mind easing,
When will I get close to you, just once,
O lord, Channamallikarjuna, jasmine-tender?

A vacana that refers to the practice of Yoga.

Antler horn: Siva the hunter is often shown with such a horn,
sometimes holding an antelope.

158

The hill is empty of content, they say;
How then are the trees born?
Coal has no essence, they say;
How then does iron melt in it?
I am bodiless, they say;
How then will Channamallikarjuna, jasmine-tender,
Love and join you?

A vacana that refers to the means of transcending the body by
fusion, through union with Siva.

159

See the wonderful way love has set its firm seal:
Arrow shot, even the feather shouldn't be seen;
Embracing, the bones should crack and powder;
Coupling, the joint should never come out;
Desire was fulfilled.
The love of Channamallikarjuna, jasmine-tender,
Was firmly fixed, O mother.

160

Stepping on the root of the primal centre,
I climbed the space in the eyebrows;
Holding on to the root of practice,
I ascended the peak of oneness;
With dispassion for a stepping stone,
I climbed the holy mountain;
Hold my hand and lift me up,
O Channamallikarjuna, jasmine-tender.

A vacana that refers to the ascent of vital energy through the cakras, common to all types of Yoga.

161

Dispassion itself is passion;
Don't call yourself dispassionate, O brother,
Till the heart of sight is cut out,
Till the earthenware of doing is all broken,
Till the eight delusions are milled and husked,
Till the doubts running between yes and no are all
   done with,
Don't call yourself dispassionate, O brother.
Channamallikarjuna, jasmine-tender,
The lord of the holy mountain,
Alone is dispassionate;
See, O brother.

162

Changing bondage into liberation,
Making the mind a diamond horse, and the soul the
    rider,
Not letting it jump up, or leap forward,
Holding back the horse close, and dragging it
    somehow to stand
still on the beautiful petal:
They don't know this
And keep slipping on the coral stone into the mire.
The jeweller does not see the shining jewel fallen
On the royal road of the marketplace,
And weeps for himself, O lord.
Over the incense burner of the prime basis,
Placing embers of the heart centre,
And stopping the wind by the breath,
The heat of that fire goes and touches the crown
    crevice;
The pot of ambrosia kept there breaks and showers
    onto the
heart centre,
Then the light of the wonderful jewel can be seen.
Who is there to know this, O lord, other than the
    egoless devotees,
The devotee who knows the here and hereafter,
And knows what the five senses need?
Only the devotee who has left the body.
All these others, killers of life,

Whoever will know you,
Other than your devotee, Basava,
O Channamallikarjuna, jasmine-tender
Lord of the holy mountain?

Bondage ... liberation: samsara and nirvana. The whole
vacana refers to the practice of Yoga.

163

The limitations of the heavy weight of births he took
    away, O mother.
The illusions of gold and land he removed, O mother.
Taking off the shame of my body,
Channamallikarjuna, jasmine-tender,
Removed the darkness of my mind
And I have gone inside him
What will you make speak, O mother?
The soul passes through many births before it
    attains human birth.

gold and land: gold (wealth), land and sex constitute the sum
total of all worldly attachments in the tradition.

164

Devotion is the cause of wisdom.
Wisdom is the great cause of devotion.
Devotion and wisdom are like the crow's eyes.
Devotion and wisdom,
O lord of my longing
Channamallikarjuna, jasmine-tender,
Are like you, yourself.

Crow's eyes: The crow turns its head from side to side, hence alternating.

165

You won't accept ritual bath from those of unmelted
    body,
You won't accept flowers from those of undissolved
    mind,
You won't accept grain offerings from those who are
    not joyful,
You won't accept the waving of lights from those
    with their wisdom-eyes unopened,
You won't accept incense smoke from those not
    pure in their hearts,
You won't accept food offerings from those who do
    not undergo transformation,
You won't accept betel leaves from those not pure in
    thought, word and deed.
You will not have being in those with heart lotuses
    unblossomed.
What did you think I have, that you loved my palm,
Tell, O Channamallikarjuna, jasmine-tender?

A vacana that refers to different stages in ritual worship.

166

The body was dedicated, the mind kept reserved,
The mood was firmly sealed.
The love of the wonderful one, agreement without
    falsehood,
When they become inseparable like soldered metal,
Channamallikarjuna, jasmine-tender,
Becomes solidified inside, O mother.

167

If one tries to break a hole in the wall in the daytime,
Because of one's haste, the hole is not made, the
    goods not stolen.
As the monkey climbing the thorn tree
Did not get the fruit, or place to sit,
I am not one who has given up everything,
Nor have I, joining you, become clanless,
O Channamallikarjuna, jasmine-tender.

Clanless: the devotee must give up all limited identities.

168

In the burnt-out ashes, I saw the ash that was not
    burnt;
Nobody knows the secret of the one
Who made the unburnt ashes into a mountain.
Knowing him, taking shelter in him, I am saved.
Seeing various things on that mountain top,
I keep moving,
O Channamallikarjuna, jasmine-tender.

169

Before knowing right and wrong
I came through many births.
Coming through them, I was hurt and burnt,
Then I came to you in faith and took refuge.
Please see that I do not stray away from you; of your
    grace,
I would beg just one thing
Please undo my binding,
Do, O Channamallikarjuna, jasmine-tender.

170

In front of man, maya
Becomes the thought 'woman'
And troubles him.
In front of woman, maya
Becomes the thought 'man'
And troubles her.
To the maya of the world,
The pure ways of the devotee
Seem foolish.
The devotee in whom
Channamallikarjuna, jasmine-tender, is pleased
Has no maya, no forgetfulness,
And no such differentiating thoughts.

171

I look at the path, thinking he has come;
When he does not, I melt in misery, O mother;
If he delays, I am ruined;
Away from Channamallikarjuna, jasmine-tender,
I become like the cakravaka bird
Separated from its mate.

Cakravaka bird: the ruddy goose or Brahmany duck, known for lifelong fidelity to its mate.

172

The mother called 'the beyond', born of space,
Gave birth to five children:
One had becoming for form, another vital breath
    for form;
The third, of five faces, took the form of the body;
Two others were the cause of creation and
    preservation.
Seeing no happiness in the palace of the five-faced one
I will go away to Kailas, won't step into the mortal
    world,
O Channamallikarjuna, jasmine-tender,
You are my witness.

Beyond … space: para in the original 'beyond', 'transcendent'; bayalu ('void') has been rendered as 'space'.

One had becoming … another vital breath for form: the original has bhava, the mind (from bhav, 'to become'), and prana, vital breath.

Five faces … body: the five senses.

Kailas: the abode of Siva, the supreme state.

173

United with the joy of the form,
The mind became known.
Where, now, will I be limbless in you?
Where, now, will I be joined to you?
Speak to me of the place where the transformation
Coming from ultimate joy
Tears down the mind's fences,
Won't you, Channamallikarjuna, jasmine-tender?

United with ... form: literally 'associating with the joy of the linga'.

Transformation: parinama, inner change arising out of understanding the real, like 'conversion' in its pure inner sense.

Tears down the mind's fences: so that the mind can transcend its bounds and identify with Siva.

174

When the Siva-linga flies off its pedestal
And comes to the palm of the hand,
To be scattered to dust in light
Which becomes ever brighter,
To be powdered to dust with body,
mind and sight fixed on the linga,
Swinging in the joy of Siva-love,
Uniting with the truly devout;
I become shameless and join you,
O Channamallikarjuna, jasmine-tender.

The overwhelming nature of the union, and its strong erotic content, are to be noted.

175

The four watches of the day
I am anxious for you.
The four watches of the night
I wane, missing you;
Day and night I remain in your desire,
Forgetting myself
O Channamallikarjuna, jasmine-tender,
Planting your love,
I have banished hunger, thirst and sleep.

176

Born in the hands of the guru,
I grew up in the kindness of innumerable devotees.
The milk of creative imagination, the ghee of right
    knowledge,
And the sugar of ultimate meaning, they fed me;
Feeding me this threefold nectar till I was full they
    brought me up.
They gave me in marriage to a husband who was as
    myself;
To send me home, the devotees all came together.
I will live there to please Basavanna.
I will take the hand of Channamallikarjuna,
    jasmine-tender.
Bring only flowers for your head, not grass,
Please go back, all you holy ones,
I bow to you.

This vacana is supposed to have been said at the time of
Akka's departure from the assembly of devotees for her final
journey to the holy mountain.

Born in the hands of the guru: reborn into the pure ways of
wisdom by initiation.

Bring only flowers ... grass: will not bring you into disrepute.

Basavanna: older brother Basava; from anna, the masculine of
akka, 'older sister'.

177

The body breaking through the linga of action
Inhered in the linga;
The mind, mixing with knowledge, serving the
    mendicant,
Inhered in the linga of the moving one.
The mood, merging with the linga of the guru,
    enjoying great grace,
Became one with the linga of the guru.
O Channamallikarjuna, jasmine-tender,
By your love, becoming differenceless,
I myself became the linga, O lord.

❦

The three lingas refered to are linga, jangama and guru; see
Introduction.

178

Clad in clothes of fire
And thrown out of the village,
I still met the friend as arranged, O mother!
In that ultimate fourth state, swinging,
Wonder-struck, impossible to stay, O mother,
Breaking up from the state, I burned in pain.
When the hill burns, leaving the tree,
And the golden bodhi tree writhes,
Channamallikarjuna, jasmine-tender,
Will condescend
To come and join me.

Ultimate fourth state: the transcendent, silent, absolute state of consciousness.

Hill burns … tree writhes: another reading is 'when the elephant burns, and the hill too, and the golden bodhi tree burns/ remains'. A reduction to pure being and verticality is perhaps meant.

179

Seeing the eternal, real state coming to me,
Memory dissolved, mind withered,
The heart blossomed.
Confined in tight bonds,
Not knowing here or there,
I leaned on the feet of
Channamallikarjuna, jasmine-tender,
In oblivion.

180

As an elephant fighting its own shadow
In the moonstone kills itself,
The way of the elephant, the mind of the elephant,
The elephant is, no, it is not.
What to say of it?
You are caught in my palm;
Why then this delusion of you and I?
There is no way I can be other than you,
Channamallikarjuna, jasmine-tender.

The apparent separation of the self from the All or Absolute
makes life an 'ignoble strife'.

181

The pearl is formed in water, the hailstone is formed
    in water.
Salt is formed in water.
Salt dissolved, hailstone dissolved,
No has seen the pearl dissolved.
These worldly men, though touching the linga,
Bear the burden of becoming,
I, reaching you, become fulfilled,
Channamallikarjuna, jasmine-tender.

Worldly men ... burden of becoming: though outwardly
religious, are not freed of their burdens.

I ... become fulfilled: kari gollu, meaning any of the following:
to burn out, merge; to become solidified, take shape.

182

If the master comes to my house today,
I will fill the vessel of my body
With the water for his feet
And pour it from my eyes;
With cooling paste of eternal peace
I will anoint him;
Knowing him to be unexpendable wealth
I will decorate him with rice grains;
Offering worship with the lotus of the heart,
Imagining the real creatively, I will offer incense;
I will wave camphor with the light of Siva-knowledge
And make food offerings, ever content.
Betel leaves of inner transformation
And the music of the five Brahmas I will offer.
I will watch with pleasure, and dance for joy,
Sing in ecstasy and join in devotion,
And play in union with the eternal.
O Channamallikarjuna, jasmine-tender,
At the feet of the guru who showed me your state,
I will melt as wax.

A vacana that describes traditional welcoming rites on the
arrival of a guru or hononured guest; see note to 156.

183

I, the child born of the love between
The impossible and the possible,
Have made a wager with the world;
I have chained by their feet
Desire, anger, greed, delusion, pride and strife.
Wafting the scent of the guru's grace,
Wearing great devotion for a beauty spot,
I will defeat and kill you
With devotion to the auspicious one for sword.
Leave, let go, karma, I won't stop till I've slain you.
Do not get destroyed, listen to my words.
Buying the sword of devotion to Siva,
I will fight and slay you.
Breaking the fetters that Brahma bound,
Shoving aside the maya of Visnu,
I will give battle; just wait till
Channamallikarjuna, jasmine-tender,
Nods his head.

The impossible and the possible: literal translations of aghatita and ghatitana.

Desire … strife: the six enemies of contemplation.

Karma: action, as well as latent potential for action, affecting realistic appraisal.

Fight and slay: a vigorous attitude is called for in acheiving the Real, or spiritual aim.

184

Ignorant people think that they have caught hold of
The formless linga in their palms –
The linga unseen by Visnu, Brahma,
The Vedas, epics and all their seeking.
For devotion there is reward, but not the linga;
For action, infernal suffering, but not the linga;
For knowledge, roaming, not the linga;
Therefore, if the self, knowing itself, becomes itself,
Channamallikarjuna, jasmine-tender, himself,
Is no other.

❧

Formless linga: refers to the impossibility of attaining to the
'pure being' of the linga by conventional means, all vitiated by
dualistic (subject–object) thinking; see Introduction.

185

Cut bamboo, will it put out shoots again?
Burnt clay pot, can it go back to earth as before?
Fallen fruit, can it join the stalk again?
Men, caught in their frustrations' toil, may speak
    without seeing,
But the devotees, firmly established, will they come
    back to the world,
Channamallikarjuna, jasmine-tender?

The path of the absolutist mystic transcends the repetitive nature
of relativistic phenomena. There are two paths: one of return,
and one of non-return, to the world.

186

What is the use of knowing everything
If one does not know the self?
When one knows in oneself
Why ask others?
Channamallikarjuna, jasmine-tender,
Yourself becoming knowledge,
You showed me the way.
I know you through yourself, O lord.

187

The sunlight seen, the dimensions of space, the
    movement of air,
The tender shoots and flowers of the six colours
Of the trees, shrubs and herbs,
Are all light-offerings of the day.
Moonlight, stars, fire, lightning and
All, worship you at night.
Day and night I remain in your worship,
Forgetting myself,
O Channamallikarjuna, jasmine-tender.

188

Rising in the morning, I think of you alone;
I wait for your coming.
Seat and canopy readied,
I await your footsteps,
O Channamallikarjuna, jasmine-tender,
Wondering when you will come.

189

If he goes to the battlefield, I will stay quiet, but
Staying in my hand, staying in my mind,
If he does not speak to me,
How can I bear it?
If memory, the go-between, doesn't make
Channamallikarjuna, jasmine-tender, love me,
What shall I do, O friend?

❀

Memory, the go-between: pure memory, free from retrospective
regret and prospective anxiety, may be meant.

190

The peacock will dance on the mountain top,
Not in some grassy patch, is that not so?
The swan will play in lakes;
Will it come, sporting in some pit?
Will the koel sing unless the mango blooms?
Will the bumblebee go to flowers without fragrance?
Will my mind go to any other than my god,
Channamallikarjuna, jasmine-tender,
Ask, O my friends?

191

Mother-in-law, she is maya;
Father-in-law, he is worldly becoming;
Three younger brothers-in-law, they are like tigers.
Four are my sisters-in-law,
Five older brothers-in-law, no god wants them.
These six sisters-in-law, I can't overcome;
Listen, and the seven maids keep watch over me.
Karma, action, is the name of my husband;
Striking him across his face, I will join Siva in love.
Through the grace of my friend called the mind
I have learned to merge in Hara, the destroyer,
Joining the handsome lord of the holy mountain,
Channamallikarjuna, jasmine-tender,
I have married a Real man.

Images involving relatives are found in many vacanas.

Three younger brothers-in-law: the qualities, modalities of nature: the pure-clear, satva; the affective-passionate, rajas; the inert-dark, tamas.

Five older brothers-in-law: the senses.

Four sisters-in-law: the four inner organs: manas, buddhi, citta and ahamkara.

Six sisters-in-law: perhaps the six enemies of contemplation, starting with desire.

192

What difference is there between
Solid and liquid ghee, O lord?
What difference is there between
A lamp and its light, O lord?
What difference is there between
Body and self, O lord?
My true body was shown by the guru
Through the initiatory chant, thus:
No difference there is between being
Embodied or being without parts, O lord.
Joining Channamallikarjuna, jasmine-tender,
I have lost my mind,
Why, then, make me talk, O lord?

193

You are the whole forest,
You are the heavenly trees of the forest,
You are the birds and beasts that play on the trees;
O Channamallikarjuna, jasmine-tender,
All-filling you are, yet
Won't show me your face?

194

It is true, the dead body called out,
The hidden desire invited,
Curdled milk turned sweet;
Verify this and see, in the lord
Channamallikarjuna, jasmine-tender.

This vacana is in the form of a riddle and its answer is in the next one.

195

195

In forgetful slumber, getting up in dream, the dead
    awoke,
The rightfully ordained, hidden treasure invited,
Curdled milk became ghee and was sweet.
Why find fault with this,
In Channamallikarjuna, jasmine-tender,
The god of gods, O brothers?

196

Well-being was the bed, glances ornaments,
Embraces clothes, and
Kisses nourishment;
Love talk was betel leaves,
The ardour of passion the unguents;
The union with Channamallikarjuna, jasmine-tender,
Is supreme felicity, O mother.

197

Better than pleasure of being together all the time,
Is the joy of love after a separation.
I can't stay apart even for a moment, my friend;
To be never parted from my lord,
Channamallikarjuna, jasmine-tender,
When will it be?

198

I would catch and hold him, but he won't be caught;
I would block him, but he will go over;
Away even for a second, I get worried.
Without seeing Channamallikarjuna, jasmine-tender,
I won't know who I am, O mother.

199

If the woman is woman, there is defilement from man,
And if the man is man, defilement from woman;
If the defilement of the mind stops,
Is there room for the defilement from the body?
The whole world is caught in this defilement,
Which was not there in the beginning, O lord;
To my god, Channamallikarjuna, jasmine-tender,
The great one, the whole world is woman.

The self as a woman in relation to the Absolute as man, or vice
versa, is found in all mystical traditions.

200

What can a barren woman know of labour pains,
Or a stepmother of fond kisses?
How can those who have known no suffering
Feel the suffering of those in pain?
The terrible pain of the broken knife of
Channamallikarjuna, jasmine-tender,
Writhing within me,
How can you ever know that, O mothers?

201

By the time the rich man opens his granary,
The poor man's life will fly away;
Till you are done with trying and testing,
Is this to be my fate, O father?
Till the wound heals,
It is as though a buffalo were swept away by the wind.
How will you show me your kindness,
O Channamallikarjuna, jasmine-tender?

202

I will go home to my village and stay there;
Once I go, I won't return this side, O mother.
Mother-in-law, father-in-law,
Older and younger brothers-in-law, nephew,
And a husband who rubs and tests the mind,
And the sister-in-law who calls me to a dark room
To eat and heaps abuse of all kinds, O mother.
Five brothers-in-law, five sisters-in-law,
Altogether they torture me:
They mock me, shout and slander me,
And hurt in all ways;
I cannot take this anymore, O mother.
My father and mother, the immortal hosts,
My mother's house, kalyana, the auspicious assembly,
Once I go near Channamallikarjuna, jasmine-tender,
The kind one of the holy hill,
I won't come back here, O mother.

Go home to my village: return to the place of origin.

203

If you plant chaff instead of rice,
Will it ever grow and give grain,
Even if irrigated with holy water?
Those without wisdom may
Observe all the rules;
Will they ever come to happiness,
Free of desire?
The scent that wafts, will it stay in one place?
Those who do not know my god
Channamallikarjuna, jasmine-tender,
Know not the way of conduct.

Observance of rules and rituals is no substitute for certitude
arising out of one's own experience, which is wisdom.